Music and the
European Mind

Music and the European Mind

By Wilfrid Dunwell

New York • THOMAS YOSELOFF

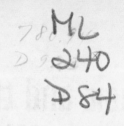

© WILFRID DUNWELL 1962

Thomas Yoseloff: Publisher
8 East 36th Street
New York 16, N. Y.

Printed in the United States of America

Preface

THE aim of this book is to present an outline of the relation of music and the other arts to the ways of life, the thought and the beliefs of the peoples of Europe. The student of music can keep a better perspective in his own art if he regards it not only as an expression of the genius of particular individuals, but of the mind and character of a wider community in successive phases of its experience. The general reader too, whether his interest is in music, or in history, or in any of the characteristics which make us the people we are, can enjoy a fuller satisfaction in his own field of interest if he sees it in its environment, and if he recalls the motives underlying conduct and the ideals which have inspired achievement. It is a truism that the arts reflect the mind of an age, and draw their sustenance from the experiences of mankind. But they give back more than they receive. Creative imagination transmutes those experiences into art which outlives the practical activities of an age, and endures as a permanent revelation of a people's aspirations. This is especially true of a civilization before it has developed its habits of intellectual and scientific inquiry; its nature at that stage is most clearly revealed through the intuitive approaches of religion and of art.

In the 20th century we are no longer disposed to make assumptions about the inevitability of progress. Since no age can claim a whole knowledge of truth, we look to each in turn for some of its aspects. Scholarship, art criticism, and a copious literature both for the specialist and the general reader have opened ranges of knowledge, and shown inexhaustible riches of artistic experience which invite our exploration in long-neglected centuries. Life and leisure are too short for any of us to fill in the picture, but a sketch of one person's impressions may help another to make his own approach. Selection and emphasis can only be personal. My hope is that the reader will be tempted, or provoked, to go directly to the creations of the European mind and find his own perspective.

I am indebted for permission to reproduce the photographs which appear in this book to the following: Mansell-Alinari, Plates 1, 9, 11; The Royal Institute of British Architects, Plates 3, 5, 6, 12, 13; The Syndics of the Fitzwilliam Museum,

Cambridge, Plate 2; The Board of Trinity College, Dublin, Plate 4; Service Commercial des Monuments Historiques, Paris, Plate 7; M. Baudet, Edition Reims Cathédrale, Reims, Plate 8; The Trustees of the British Museum, Plate 10; Verlag Traute Lehmann, Bamberg, Plate 14; Langewiesche Nachfolger, Hans Köster, Königstein im Taunus, from the Blauen Buch "Deutscher Barock" by Wilhelm Pinder, Plates 15, 16, 18, and from the volume "Neresheim" of the Langewiesche Bücherei, Plate 17; Verlag Schnell und Steiner, Munich, Plates 19, 20; New South Wales Government Office, Plate 21.

W. D.

Contents

List of Illustrations

Author's Note

ALTHOUGH this book is concerned with the relation of music to the wider mind of Europe, it presents an outline of purely musical developments which can be found on the following pages: 22-3, 25, 36-8, 47-50, 53, 62-3, 66-7, 101-27, 129-31, 136, 148-62, 163, 169-71, 172, 173, 180-6, 188-94, 196.

1

Art and Society

I

FEW people can have entered a cathedral without reflecting on its dual aspect, as a work of art and as a place of worship. My own memory of a small and beautiful church in Bruges is inseparable from that of a woman who came in with her shopping-basket, lifted her child on to a kneeler, prayed for a while and departed. A medieval cathedral can make its effect simply as an artistic creation, but it was built to exercise various religious and social functions. Apart from these uses, it was a symbol of ecclesiastical majesty and of the communal pride of a feudal and burgher society. Its stained-glass windows conveyed a religious message to those who could not read; its carvings commemorated the mighty or perpetuated the droll fantasies of the sculptor. Much of the music which we hear in concerts and broadcasts formerly served practical needs: Bach's Cantatas in the Lutheran service, Mozart's Divertimenti in social entertainment. The pictures we see in our art-galleries once formed part of the natural furnishing of churches and palaces, enhancing the significance and emotional appeal of religious worship and the splendour of a way of life. Being so integrated with society they are expressions of its "mind", as much as are philosophical and scientific systems, or the actions and movements which produce historical events.

Art critics are careful to distinguish between the aesthetic effect of a work of art and its social origin and purpose. Speculations about the relation of cave-drawings to the life of their creators is a separate matter from appreciation of the drawings themselves. It is so at any rate in retrospect; it may not have been for the Neolithic artist himself. In the earliest phases of civilization, art was closely related to magic, religion, and ritual; music and poetry and life were inseparable in the recounting of heroic achievements in epic form, or expression of personal emotion in folk-song. It is only when surviving works and written records perpetuate the creations of the past that an awareness of "art" emerges as something which can be appreciated in its own right, apart from its social function. The creative mind is not content with repetition. The ever-new developments in music during the long centuries of medieval monastic life show how the stimulus of artistic creation was at work, although the religious purpose remained unchanged. A steady transformation was effected by the play of the artistic mind on the materials of music itself. Awareness of artistic principles is still more acute when social and mental attitudes are changing. Italian architects of the Renaissance were highly conscious of matters of style as they turned to their Classical heritage for guidance and inspiration. In absorbing its multiform details, admiring its sureness of taste and of method, and feeling the moving power of its beauty, they were fortified in their conception of art as a world of experience with its own laws and its own imaginative visions. This enthusiasm, shared by sculptors, painters, and poets, encouraged the "professional" view of art, and, more still, the realization that creative genius can transcend the general mind of an age, while ministering to its needs and depending on its patronage. For some three or four centuries, during which creations of beauty were valued for their contribution to prestige, the interests of artist and patron coincided. The transition to democratic and industrial ways of life disturbed this balance. Art now has no general social function; its cultivation has become a highly specialized activity, and its appreciation is limited to the relatively few.

Appreciation is subject to change as much as social customs and artistic styles. At the present time, when art is so little integrated with the prevailing way of life, critical detachment prevails. The enthusiasm of the Renaissance, the self-assurance of the 18th century, the belief in progress of the 19th century have given way to an eclectic attitude, a desire to seek artistic significance in the products of any stage of civilization. The critic who applies this exclusively artistic criterion does not ask *what* the artist has done but *how* he has done it. He uses the word "significance" in preference to "beauty", since the latter word can mean widely different things to different people. To move from room to room in a museum or art-gallery is to experience the vital impact which is made by all art, not simply that of one period. One person may find his ideal of beauty in the serene harmony of a Greek vase or statue, another in the clear-cut outlines of a Byzantine mosaic. The tastes may differ, but the power to communicate aesthetic experience resides in the artistic creations themselves.

Another issue arises if we move on through the art-gallery and say: This picture conveys a feeling of spiritual ecstasy, or that one, poignant suffering. For many people, this is the essential feature of the painting. For the critic who is applying a purely aesthetic criterion, the emotional "content" of the picture is something quite separate from its "significant form". The painter's task is to reconcile both these elements, to represent what he sees in nature and human experience, and at the same time achieve the formal order which gives his work the quality of art. A similar situation arises in music, although musical sounds do not represent anything in nature. Music has often been described as a language of the emotions, but on purely aesthetic grounds it would be more accurate to define it as the art of giving significant order to sounds. Thus, a piece of music may be significant through its emotional and expressive meaning, or purely through the musical organization of its sounds. As it happens, music served a long apprenticeship as a means of communicating thought external to itself before it acquired the forms of order which made it significant in its own right. From the ancient intoning of chants and heroic lays to the complicated mingling of voices in polyphony, it was almost exclusively a vehicle for words—music for dancing was the only exception, and here too the organization was imposed from without. Through these associations music gathered the emotional connotations which now seem inseparable from its nature; but in all cases it must have its own significant order, and this can exist without any attendant "meaning".

Whether we value a work of art for its "pure" significance or for its emotional content is a matter of personal temperament, taste, and training. It is obviously possible to combine the two approaches. But as soon as we consider the subject-matter of art we are brought into contact with the thought and experiences of the artist and his environment. Our appreciation is enhanced by understanding his aims and mental outlook. And since the urge to artistic creation is restricted to no time and place, and no stage of civilized development, we shall find art which has significant value at any one of these stages. Social life shows evolution from simple to complex forms; this in itself is not a criterion of value. Art, as an expression of that social life, may show a parallel evolution, but this does not necessarily affect its value; it may be good or bad at any stage. Evolution therefore, in the sense of progress, has no relevance to art in its social aspects. It has relevance, however, to the development of the resources of art itself, and these can make possible artistic experiences which would not otherwise be attainable. Thus there are two ways of comparing our reaction to a simple work like a folk-song and a composite one like a symphony. The first is to realize that each is a unique thing, giving perfect aesthetic satisfaction. What comparison is possible between such different things? This is the judgment of the aesthetic purist. The second (which would be that of the hypothetical "reasonable man" who is such a useful legal fiction) is to recognize that the symphony opens up ranges of thought and of emotion which are not possible in a folk-song: the fascinating interrelations of a great musical structure, the contrasts of mood, of tension and repose, and the added richness of orchestral sonority and colour. One is not better than the other, but the symphony is the result of a process of evolution without which these varied experiences would be unattainable. The difference is not merely one of size. A long symphony does not necessarily offer richer experience than a short one, although it may need ampler space in which to develop its implications. The difference is one of quality: a symphony can do what a folk-song does not set out to do. This is to labour the obvious, but it is a necessary qualification of the view which would dismiss the whole conception of artistic evolution. This was perhaps a natural attitude at a time when historical research was beginning to throw light on periods which were remote and neglected. There is no longer reason to fear that any part of our cultural heritage will be underestimated.

There is more cause for misgiving in a superficial view which has a certain currency, that all the arts share common characteristics in every age. This gives rise to misleading and tendentious naming of periods ("Renaissance Music") and to attributions to one art of qualities which are distinctive of another. It also assumes that the arts keep step with one another in their respective technical developments, that for example the music of Pérotin is comparable with the architecture of Notre-Dame de Paris in which it was performed. Such notions have no relevance to the actual historical development and the richly varied characters of the European peoples.

II

Art makes its impact on society because it springs from the deeper levels where human beings share a common nature. The artist differs from the craftsman in experiencing an emotional urge which drives him to creative activity. He cannot dispense with the craftsman's technical experience; the Gothic cathedral builders saw the collapse of many of their central towers before this truth was learnt. Like the craftsman, the artist must have the skill to control and give order to the material elements of his medium; manual and mental activities contribute largely to this technical end. But there is one aspect of the achievement of order which lies deeper than technique in the sense of acquired skill. The human mind is constantly receiving impressions through the senses, and that part of it which we call memory is not by any means fully under our conscious control. Impressions are stored, and with or without our will they interact with one another to produce new combinations and so become part of a total amalgam of experience. It is from these sources that the artist derives the germinal ideas which are the basis of his finished creation. Every person differs from every other in the sum of his experiences and in his powers of absorption. Every person also shares some common characteristics with other members of the community to which he belongs. An audience of Europeans listening to a Beethoven symphony will show different degrees of response as individuals, but as a group they will share a common understanding of that particular musical convention. Not so a group of Oriental listeners. Their store of impressions has been built up within conventions which exclude the European one.

The artistic convention then is a form of order which creative minds achieve, partly by conscious technical means, partly by preliminary, involuntary shaping processes taking place below the conscious level. The extent of this conscious effort differs of course with different artists; Beethoven's sketch-books show the actual processes of work, stage by stage, while Schubert's spontaneity is a byword. But whatever the degree of conscious technique in the achievement of order, there can be no doubt that the emotional urge which is the driving force impelling the artist to create comes from a still deeper source, from the volcano as it were which exists in the depths of every human personality. This substratum expresses itself, at the lowest level, in animal instincts and passions which demand satisfaction. The normal individual finds release for them in personal relationships, and his super-abundant energies may expend themselves in sport, play, and hobbies. The outlet for more assertive types may be in competitive activities like war, politics, business. For other types the outlet may be found in intellectual pursuits which drive them to an output of energy far beyond the minimum required for comfortable living. These activities all stem from the vital need each person feels to fulfil his personality, to achieve, to be potent.

A new factor comes into play in the case of the artist. He not only shows himself capable of doing, but of achieving style in his manner of doing. This is one of the ways in which he surpasses the craftsman. He not only creates, but he creates a unique thing, which has significance because of his creative imagination. Within him a germinal idea lies latent, he is driven by an emotional urge to develop it, he has the technical skill to communicate it, and a work of art comes into existence. But this is not the end. He lives in a community whose members have grown up with experiences similar to his own. They share his emotional urge to express, in some degree or other; they have a store of impressions which is bound to coincide with his at many points, and when they are in the presence of his finished work of art, which brings their own aspirations to a focus, they are drawn to identify themselves with the artist and enjoy the vicarious satisfaction of creation. The artistic experience completes itself in the emotional response of the recipient. Herein lies the power of art, in the subtle relationship between creator and would-be creator. Through his superior imagination the artist gives new interpretation to the ordinary experiences of life, and so enlarges the vision of all who receive his communication. He does so, not as teacher or preacher at the intellectual level, but by a flash of illumination which reveals to the ordinary man the height and depth of his nature. The artist touches us in the most intimate regions of our experience. We cannot all achieve power and success, or dazzle with intellect or beauty, but we all do experience desires and disappointments, joys and sorrows. We all in some degree feel our helplessness in a world of strange chances. Some take confidence from the religious conception of a world transcending this mortal one. But in art, the very fears and trials of this present world are transmuted into beauty and raised to a plane where individual suffering loses its merely personal application.

The artist's value to a community then lies in the gifts which he brings to it through his imagination, surpassing the merely useful, and so contributing to the permanent heritage of civilization. Precious and individual as are these gifts, the artist depends in one essential respect on the society in which he lives. Whatever his latent ability he cannot develop it in isolation. Corporate tradition is the basis of his craft, public demand gives the opportunity for its exercise. The ideas and ideals of a community dictate the forms and framework within which the artist works. He endows them with artistic significance, but he depends on them in the first place for the direction taken by his own thoughts and intuitions. He also depends on society for the physical means to express these thoughts in terms of his own particular art. He needs materials and labour for his buildings and their adornment, and increasingly elaborate resources for the performance of his music. These material needs have always been provided by church or court, by municipality or private patron for the furtherance of their ideals or the attainment of an ampler way of living. Under these conditions the artist can bring his work to fruition; failing such environment, his genius must lie dormant. The cultural life of Europe is the story of countless partnerships of this kind between artist and society.

2

Christianity and the End of the Ancient World

THE peoples of Europe are diverse in language and character, but none the less they possess a fundamental unity which derives from the power of ideas and beliefs held in common. These spring from two sources, the Christian religion and the civilization of ancient Greece. The European mind owes its special character to the interaction of these two influences, and its cultural tradition begins at the time when they first made their joint impact on the peoples surrounding the Mediterranean. This was in the period following the recognition of Christianity by the Emperor Constantine in A.D. 313 and its establishment some ten years later as the official religion of the Roman Empire. Only then could the Church come into the open and begin to develop its organization, build and adorn its churches, and elaborate its ritual and music; only then could an outlet be found for modes of thought and belief which had been taking place in secret and in isolated centres.

Christianity was born in the Hellenistic world which had taken shape after the conquests of Alexander the Great in the 4th century B.C. and which still maintained its character under Roman rule from the 2nd century B.C. It was a world of trading cities, some of them vast and crowded, founded at points of communication by Greek and Macedonian soldiers, and bearing the imprint of the older civilization of Greece. Although the spirit of Hellas had departed, the external forms were evident in the election of magistrates, in gymnastic and religious festivals, in performance of Classical dramas, and in the welcome extended to wandering sophists, rhetoricians and musicians. The language of the upper classes was Greek, and so was the material background of building, decoration, and dress. It is true that in the large centres alien influences crowded in; ignorant and superstitious populations in large masses had formed no part of the Greek conception of life. But in one vital respect posterity owes the greatest of debts to this cosmopolitanism and widened range.

A new reading public, an increasingly systematized education based on the work of Plato and Aristotle, painstaking commentary on the masterpieces of the past conducted by learned specialists centred round the great libraries of Alexandria and Pergamum, ensured the preservation of the texts of Classical Greece. Philosophical schools and learned academies provided the equivalent of our University education. They formed the minds of men of letters or of action, like Cicero, Horace, Marcus Antonius, Julius Caesar, so making possible the Classical culture of Rome, and they further perpetuated the Greek tradition through the work of scholars, notably Arabian, whose activities were not interrupted by the later barbarian invasions of Europe.

The tradition descending from Greece of the 5th and 4th centuries B.C. runs like a vein of gold through the life of later centuries. "Almost everything which is to be valued in modern civilization is owing to the ancient culture of that part of the Mediterranean world which spoke and thought in Greek—our science and philosophy, our epic and drama and lyric poetry, our standards in sculpture and architecture, our medicine and mathematics, our theory of humane education, the form of our Christian theology, and the ideal of the rule of law which distinguishes Western civilization. The Greeks loved beauty and pursued reason. They lived close to nature. Their taste in art was austere and simple. They thought greatly about great things." (H. A. L. Fisher, *A History of Europe*.) These achievements of the Greek mind rest on the foundation of their sense of the dignity of man. Says Fisher: "The Greeks escaped the paralysing control of an organized priestcraft." Plato's conception of an ideal world, of which humanity can only perceive the shadows, was a challenge to attain as nearly as possible by human effort to the conditions of that world—the true reality. Harmony with the ideal, the true excellence of the soul, lay in a sublime moderation which is identical with wisdom and virtue. This harmony included a love of beauty and order. In the education of youth, the aim was to identify the good man with the good citizen, and the good with the beautiful. Education in art was held to be education in character.

This belief in the powers of the human mind, and the possibility of attaining spiritual harmony through philosophical inquiry, persisted long after the great Classical period of artistic creation had come to an end. The Academy of Athens survived for a thousand years until its suppression in A.D. 529 by Justinian, and similar centres of teaching and discussion perpetuated the tradition of rational search in matters of thought and conduct. Plato's conception of an ideal world transcending the temporal and physical one retained its germinal power throughout subsequent history, and its influence, through Zeno's philosophy known as Stoicism, and later through Philo and Plotinus in Neo-Platonism, was central in the shaping of Christian theology. The emphasis on conduct and thought, governed by man's relationship with an ideal world beyond the sensory one, appealed to the best minds of the Hellenistic age, and it gave an intellectual as well as a moral content to the new Christian religion.

The best minds in any age, however, are always in a minority. The large populations crowded together in cities like Alexandria were untouched by philosophy. Rather were they attracted by magic and superstition. They lived in conditions of chaos resulting from war, tyrannical government and uncertainty of food supplies. The prevailing mood was one of fatalism; fear of impending doom darkened their lives. Such people were naturally prone to respond to emotional appeal, and it was through the promise of salvation to all, regardless of class or station, that Christianity made its converts among these despairing masses. Belief in magical powers attached to food and ceremonial rites is widespread, and in the early Church the sacraments of baptism and of the Lord's Supper induced conditions of ecstasy, and satisfied a popular craving for mystery and emotional excitement. By gradual stages the Church ultimately evolved its distinctive ceremony, the Mass, refining the cruder emotions aroused by primitive rites, but still retaining the element of.mystery and belief in the actual presence of God. As the focal point of worship, and being charged with emotional significance, the service of the Mass was especially suitable for artistic development, and it ultimately became an elaborate ritual, enhanced above all by music.

The early Christians were little distinguished from Jews. Apart from belief, there was no sharp break with old forms of religion. Converted synagogue musicians continued the Jewish method of cantillation or recitation of Scripture which made use of traditional formulas, and the body of Christian chant thus came to incorporate ancient melodic features which were to remain with it and leave their permanent mark on its character. Jewish psalmody, with its free rhythm and melismatic flights of melody, made a strong impact on the Hellenistic world, in which a metrical and syllabic style of word-setting prevailed. In the early Christian Church a soloist recited the psalm on a monotone with inflections added at salient points, and the congregation interjected responses at the ends of verses. Comparatively simple in its early stages, this recitation had already become elaborate by the time of St. Augustine (354-430), who referred to the "jubili", or alleluia chants, as the summit of religious ecstasy. The whole body of unmetrical unison melody which came to be known as Plainsong owes its origin to the emotional impulses and co-operative experiences of these early forms of worship. It owes its artistic development to the conditions which favoured ecclesiastical expansion in the three centuries which followed the recognition of Christianity in the Empire.

Long before this, in the time of St. Paul, Christianity had gained a footing in Rome, from which its influences radiated, though its activities were necessarily secret, since the early Christians were suspected of subversive tendencies and were not always of the most socially respectable standing. Here they came in contact with the pagan world which was to determine the outward form of the Church's life, in architecture and the visual arts, for the rest of its history. At first, their services were held in the Catacombs, and there, in the form of wall-paintings, are to be found the first examples of early Christian pictorial art. These were conservative in style and technique, since they were executed by painters familiar with the current domestic art of the Romans, and conservative even in the acceptance of pagan subject-matter. Painting in fact was rather regarded as a secret language than as an art, as for example in the use of the Classical figure of Apollo as a symbol representing Christ. Under the stress of persecution the new religion could find little outlet for an artistic expression of its own.

The situation was transformed when Constantine chose Christianity as his personal cult and when it became the official religion of the Empire. A great period of church building and decoration began in the 4th century. Once again the Christian religion adopted existing forms. These were of great splendour, for the Romans had high constructive ability, and their architecture reflected the grandeur of their power and the lavish patronage of a succession of emperors from Augustus (died A.D. 14) to Diocletian (died 305). They had inherited the legacy of Greece and that of the Etruscans, a sensitive artistic people of Central Italy who had been active between 750 and 100 B.C. The former bequeathed the example of their perfectly proportioned temples, with columns supporting horizontal slabs and entablatures, and the latter added the arch, dome, and vault of ultimate Eastern origin. Guided by these models the Romans applied their own structural genius to produce a wealth of buildings for their practical purposes, temples, amphitheatres, baths, aqueducts, bridges, tombs, and basilicas. Apart from the immediate influence on Christian building in the 4th century, there are few places in Europe to-day which do not possess some building of this Graeco-Roman character, most probably inspired by the Renaissance revival of this ancient art.

The basilicas provided the model in the first stages of Christian building. They were the law-courts and commercial centres of the Romans. Their form was rectangular, with either two or four rows of columns, and above were usually upper galleries with columns supporting the roof. At the end was a semicircular apse, which was roofed with a semi-dome. Here, raised on a dais, had been the tribunal, separated from the main building by a screen of columns, or a balustrade, in front of which was the altar where sacrifice was offered before transacting business. The appropriateness of this architectural form for Christian worship is obvious: the eye is carried along the line of columns to the focal point of the service at the altar. As ritual developed, the choir in front of the altar was enclosed by low screen walls or "cancelli" (hence "chancel"), and an "ambo" or pulpit was provided on either side from which the Gospel and Epistle were read. (See Plate 1.) Frequent movements of the officiating clergy between these various points required appropriate music, which differed in character from that suitable for the more devotional and sacrificial moments of the Mass. The form of the music developed in response to the needs of the liturgy. It is in fact impossible to consider the music of the Mass as an art-form in itself; it is only a portion of a larger ritual, which, apart from its religious significance, can be regarded as a composite artistic experience.

Before the passing of the ancient world the Church had called into her service three arts which are now a living part of our Western culture. They had their roots in the older civilizations, both Oriental and European, but they belong to our world since they are dominated by the Christian religion. In this, they provide a striking example of the two aspects under which art may be observed. They served a purpose which is external to art—that of religion—but each of them in these years from 300 to 600 achieved a state of perfection in the pure realm of art. Plainsong, as a cultivated art of unaccompanied melody, remains unsurpassed in beauty; Byzantine mosaics, like those in the Mausoleum of Galla Placidia in Ravenna, give the highest aesthetic satisfaction through pure form and colour; early Christian and Byzantine churches, which include the supreme triumph of domical structure in S. Sofia (537) at Constantinople, have their own unique quality as art.

The Church had by now achieved a temporal as well as a spiritual power, and these arts reflected its glory. The music, with its emotional and mysterious quality, enhanced by its Oriental character, was supremely fitted to be the vehicle for the central rite of the faith and the expression of its spiritual aspirations. The buildings, and the majestic forbidding figures of the mosaics, on the other hand, spoke rather of a divine authority than of a saviour's compassion. They were symbols too of a dominating ecclesiastical power. In its earliest days Christianity had brought into human experience an attitude hitherto unknown. The idea of a sympathetic relationship among men, and between God and man, had not been prevalent in a world of priestly and kingly authority, where the propitiation of supernatural powers by sacrifice was the prevailing motive. Neither had it been the ruling principle in Greek thought, which gave pre-eminence to an ordered and balanced mode of conduct. While drawing elements from both these conceptions, Christianity made its magnetic appeal through its message of divine love and its emphasis on the worth of each individual soul. Once established in the Empire, however, the Church developed her external organization on the Roman model, becoming a worldly as well as a spiritual power, and now in the 6th century when political command had passed to invaders from the north, she found herself the only stable institution which could survive the disruptions and destructions of the Dark Ages. Before that night descended, she had called the contemporary arts into her service, charged them with a new emotion, and created the environment for the first great flowering of European art.

3

The Dark Ages and the Northern Races

IN the years between 500 and 1000 the focus of Western life was moving away from the Mediterranean to the north-west of Europe, where peoples of different temperament were to receive the Classical and Christian heritages, and in assimilating them create a distinctive culture of their own. The European mind was formed in the process of absorbing this tradition, and new civilized values were to emerge from the interaction of ancient thought and fresh racial character.

The first stages of this process were violent. Already by the 3rd century internal decay was at work in the Roman Empire; external pressures of migrating peoples completed the disintegration, and by the end of the 5th century separate barbarian chieftains were ruling in the kingdoms of Italy, Spain, Gaul, and North Africa. Nominal allegiance continued to be paid in Italy to the Eastern Emperor at Constantinople, and Byzantine influences continued to penetrate to the West along the trade routes, through centres like Venice, Ravenna, and Marseilles. Permanent fruits of this influence survive to-day in the mysterious beauty of St. Mark's, Venice, and the churches and the mosaics of Ravenna. But preservation was not the key-note of the period of the invasions, as successive waves of Teutonic and other peoples rolled westward from Asia until the 10th century. The names of the earliest, Huns and Vandals, have become synonymous with barbarism and destruction; the Gothic peoples bore a name which to a later civilization called up all that was uncouth and inharmonious. The Franks, Allemans, Lombards, Angles, Saxons, Northmen, have given their name and racial character to the nations of modern Europe, but at their first impact on the Western and Mediterranean world it seemed that all that was of civilized value had perished for ever. Wars and changes of political rule had been familiar experiences in the ancient world, but they had never brought about the obliteration of all centres of learning, or interrupted the tradition of culture and ideas.

Now, in the 5th and 6th centuries, the educated world of the Mediterranean was overrun and the continent of Europe inhabited by races of men who were completely ignorant save for the songs and tales of their own warlike exploits, and the forms of art which are characteristic of primitive peoples.

In disrupting ancient civilization and obliterating many of the products of its genius the invasions wrought irreparable damage. But civilizations do not retain their creative power for ever; there was little evidence of positive force and self-renewal during the last two or three centuries of the Empire, and in the broad perspective of European history, immeasurable gains flowing from the influx of races far outweighed the immediate losses. Enough remained of Roman organization for some of the new peoples to be settled before the Empire collapsed, and as the Church, with her steadily increasing power, perpetuated well-tried methods of provincial government, the first stages of chaos gave way at length to a general condition of stability. Barbarian ignorance too yielded to educative method, and the distinctive mind of Europe was able to reveal itself soon after the first millennium.

The period which preceded that awakening has interest not so much for the intrinsic value of its own achievements as for the light it throws on salient features which distinguish European from any other civilization. Its own social organization, broadly based on the feudal system of overlordship through tenure of land, and on monastic centres amid rural populations, has passed away; the system of education which emerged, after the initiative of Charlemagne, was necessarily restricted to the most primitive needs, and, even so, it was directed chiefly to religious ends; the pattern of towns and trade-routes which began to take shape when relative peace was attained at the end of the 10th century; all these formed an environment which has little in common with that of modern Europe. The arts, as will be seen, were conservative in character, and the vernacular languages were still evolving from their parent Latin and Germanic stocks. It is not for these contemporary, external features that the age is interesting, but for the opportunity it presents of observing some of the defining traits of an emerging civilization. The very sparseness of event in these centuries sharpens the contrast between ancient civilizations and the European one which was coming to life.

Three notable characteristics became apparent. One is the energetic pioneering spirit which brought the invading races here in the first place, and has led them ever since to exploration and settlement throughout the world. Their "outward-going" mentality differs markedly from the contemplative, static mind of Oriental peoples. Accompanied by active powers of organization it has led in the course of our history to the continuous search for new horizons and environments, and an ever-widening range of scope and interest which includes people of all stations and ways of thought. The all-embracing character of medieval life and art, the bourgeois and domestic detail of Dutch and Flemish painting, the readiness of 20th-century artists, writers, musicians, to include the sordid, the macabre, the unusual in any form, as subjects for artistic treatment, all spring from this exploring spirit. They all contribute to a view of life and art which has a totally different emphasis from such ancient hieratic and imperial cultures as those of Babylon, Egypt, Byzantium, or the classical Greek conception of the balanced and idealized man.

A second characteristic is a delight in complex structure. The European makes things. In modern times he has fallen into an industrial way of life and shows little sign of being content with knowledge for its own sake. The ancient Greeks too had insatiable curiosity, shown in scientific as well as philosophic inquiry, but the average European is not concerned with pure thought; he must needs apply the discoveries of science to practical ends. This is obvious in the modern world, in the ramifications of organized society and in the complexities of the physical machinery on which we have come to depend. It is, no less, a characteristic which distinguishes our art, architecture, music, and literature. It is enough to mention the intricacies of Gothic architecture and the elaborate combinations of our part-singing and orchestral music. Eastern music shows subtlety in melodic organization, African music in rhythmic elaboration, but neither approaches the all-embracing complexity of a European symphony, either in form or in the diversity of forces used. This is not advanced as a claim to superiority; it is an indication of a typical Western habit of mind. It is a quality which appears in our art, whether that art is appreciated for its pure form or as an expression of emotional and intellectual experiences.

A third characteristic is the contrast between north and south which became a permanent feature of European life. Climatic variations played little part in Mediterranean civilization, but they impose sharply different conditions on peoples bordering the northern shores. Architecture shows most directly the effect of physical environment, in the steeper pitch of roofs in the north to throw off rain and snow, and the wider window spaces to admit the sunlight which the southerner often needs to exclude. Character and temperament are equally affected. The northerner is often inclined to impute indolence and softness to his southern neighbours. Perhaps he is unjust; but our cultural history does reveal a broad tendency to intellectual effort in the north and sensuous delight in the south. The Protestant and Catholic forms of religion show the divergence clearly. To enter a Dutch cathedral is to see at a glance the difference between two worlds: within a medieval edifice which, before the Reformation, would be rich with all that the arts could offer but now is a bare shell of stone, a square of pews in tiers will surround a preacher whose sermon is the high-light of the service. Intellectual exposition is dear to the Protestant north; simple acceptance of a mystic communion in an atmosphere of beauty is the way of the south. These two attitudes influence the artistic as well as the religious life of Europe, at all stages of its history. Contrapuntal textures in music—interchange of ideas, as it were—have generally developed in the north, while singing melody has its natural home in the south; the realistic painting of the Dutch has its counterpart in the sensuous colours and forms of Renaissance Italy.

These three broad strands run through the civilization which was to emerge in Europe. They are only a part of the complex whole, but they are enough to indicate that the tribal invasions which brought to an end the world of Greece and Rome were something other than a negative force of destruction. They bore the seeds of new life. A period of darkness certainly intervened between the ancient and the medieval worlds, but it was one in which roots were forming, and in which the newcomers learnt to turn their energies from aimless destruction to purposeful creation.

Four main powers exercised political command and influenced the manner of life during most of this period of transition: the Eastern Empire, the forces of Islam, the Roman Papacy, and the northern kings. The rule of the Emperor at Constantinople provided the eastern bulwark of Christian Europe until the end of the Middle Ages. In doing so, it not only preserved a geographical frontier; it ensured the survival of the literary heritage of ancient Greece. Its own literature was pedantic, and consisted not in creative work, but in copying, and in producing lexicons and commentaries. It is fortunate that it was not original, for it

servilely retained the words of the immortal Greeks, and so was
able ultimately to transmit them to posterity. But that was far
away in the future. The immediate Byzantine influence was an
artistic one. By the end of the reign of Justinian, who died in
565, an essentially Christian art had grown to maturity which
incorporated certain Oriental features, of Syrian and Persian
origin. Intense emotional expression was the aim of this art, and
it used certain technical devices such as wide-open, staring eyes,
enlargement of heads, frontal rigid poses, harsh and brilliant
colours, to convey the inner import and feeling of the subject.
Its influence on European pictorial art lasted until the early
Renaissance. (See Plate 3.) Byzantine pictorial art had also
absorbed, from late Roman practice, panoramic landscape with
architectural features as backgrounds, and these, along with its
conventional treatment of Bible stories and Christian symbolism
were to remain prominent features in subsequent Christian art.
They were applied not only in large-scale decoration of churches,
tombs, and monuments, but with especial effect in ivory carvings
and illumination of manuscripts. Christian music, too, underwent an elaborate development in the Eastern Church (which
survives now as the Greek, or Orthodox Church). The Byzantine
liturgy came into being with Justinian, and music came to
dominate it in services of increasing splendour. A common
Semitic origin is postulated for Byzantine and Gregorian Chant,
and there was some contact between the Eastern and Western
Churches, notably through St. Ambrose, Bishop of Milan (374–97).
But the Eastern Church pursued its own course, and its music has
an interest which is separate from that of the main stream of
Western music.

Islam, the second of the ruling forces of this age, came into
being with startling suddenness in the 7th century. Born of the
mystical ardour, the vision and shrewd practical sense of
Mohamet (c. 570–632), it rapidly spread, by the power of the
sword and through its apt accommodation to the ways of desert
peoples, from its home in Arabia, over North Africa to Spain in
the west, and through the Middle East as far as the Punjab in
the north of India. It has left no permanent mark of its power
or culture in our civilization except for the architectural beauties
which were the fruit of its sojourn in Spain, but it contributed
in two important respects to the forming of the Western mind.
First, it constituted a challenge through its military pressure and
its non-Christian character which stimulated the energies of the

European nations and gave them for the first time a consciousness of unity through the idea of Christendom. This was not evident in the earliest phase, when the defence of both east and west depended on the prowess of individual leaders. The successful defence of Constantinople by Leo the Isaurian in 717 and 718, and the final stemming of the Saracen advance in the west by Charles Martel at Poitiers in 732, were individual achievements, and this phase was to provide the material for the first real literature in the vernaculars, extolling heroes like Roland, the Cid, and Charlemagne. The conception of a confraternity of nations, a militant Christendom, only became apparent at the close of this era, when Europe passed to the offensive in the Crusades. Second, the civilization of Islam, like that of Constantinople, preserved elements of Greek culture through its occupation of the old centres of the Hellenistic world (notably in science and medicine, and the work of Aristotle) which were to enter the European mind at the dawn of the High Middle Ages and completely alter its perspective. Apart from these directly educative contributions, the new Oriental culture continued to exercise a fascination for the European, and enrich him both in mind and in the amenities of life throughout the rest of history.

The third and fourth of the ruling powers of this age, the Roman papacy and the northern kings, determined the political and social organization of Europe itself. By the end of the 6th century the Church was as powerful, in purely temporal matters, as any prince, and through the single-minded purpose of successive occupants of the Holy See, and through its power of excommunication, a formidable weapon in a superstitious age, it could initiate policies whose repercussions travelled far beyond their immediate time and place. Two examples are notable, not for their intrinsic interest but because they explain some curious anomalies which persisted through most of European history. In 731, at a time of papal conflict with the Eastern Emperor on the iconoclastic issue, alliance with the neighbouring Lombard monarchy could have brought peace and unity to Italy—but perhaps at the cost of Rome's becoming an independent bishopric. The papal choice was rather to appeal to the powerful Franks for aid, and collaboration first with Pepin and later with Charlemagne ensured the expansion of the Papal State and its survival, in a divided Italy, until the 19th century. A similar collaboration with Otto I, when that Saxon warrior was crowned as Emperor in 962 established the Holy Roman Empire, an over-ambitious conception which coincided with no political reality, and left Germany three hundred years later to become, and remain until the 19th century, an anarchical federation of principalities. The political idealist might regret these confusing tangles and their trail of wars and intrigues. The student of Western culture must admit that the arts in Europe have owed an incalculable debt to the patronage of many of these princelings who adopted the trappings of a vastly exaggerated power.

Princeling is not the name to apply to some of the leading figures of the Dark Ages, whether popes, kings, or emperors. Many were simply fighting men in an age of violence—Clovis, Charles Martel, Pepin, Charlemagne himself, Henry the Fowler, Otto I, but they established Europe as a geographical entity within which a new civilization could grow. Popes like Gregory the Great, Leo IV, and Hildebrand ensured the universality of an ecclesiastical organization which, with all its faults, was the source of the astonishing spiritual and cultural life of the Middle Ages. The foundations of that life were laid at the beginning of the 9th century with Charlemagne's ambition to create a Christian empire. The campaign of 773 which took him to Rome had opened his mind to the wonders of that city, with its wealth of churches, its ritual, its Gregorian chant. He was impressed by its ordered priesthood, and being aware of the need to combat the external pressures of Islam and the internal weaknesses of chaos and ignorance, he readily accepted the Imperial crown from Pope Leo III on Christmas Day, 779. Even before that event he had begun to use his great authority to consolidate his wide domains on a Christian basis. He needed for this purpose parish priests who could read their Bible, bishops who could administer a diocese, and a church which could provide him with civil servants. In 782 he invited Alcuin from York to become head of the Palace School at Aachen.

This appointment is a landmark in the transmission of knowledge from the old world to the new. As the doctrines of Christianity had first been developed in a world dominated by pagan thought and literature, one of the chief concerns of the early Fathers of the Church had been to select and prescribe materials which were suitable for Christian education and to exclude those which might bear a pagan or heretical taint. The encyclopaedic works of Martianus Capella, Cassiodorus, Isidore of Seville, largely implemented this programme, and all were popular in

1. Basilica of S. Clemente, Rome.
4th century, rebuilt 1084-1108

2. Archbishop and sing-
ing Deacons. 9th cen-
tury ivory panel. (Fitz-
william Museum,
Cambridge.)

3. The Apse, Monreale Cathedral, Sicily. 1174.

the Middle Ages. So too were the writings of Boethius (*c.* 470–525), whose work was philosophical rather than theological. He transmitted, in far from complete form, Aristotle's logical work, which served the thinkers of the West from the 7th to the later 12th centuries, and he took up from Martianus Capella the classification of the seven liberal arts in the *trivium* (grammar, rhetoric, and logic) and the *quadrivium* (the sciences of arithmetic, astronomy, geometry, and music). The latter were concerned with the acquisition of knowledge, the former with the ordering of experience. The main value of these works is in their provision of an educational ideal which was practical, after the severing of direct links with the Classical tradition. The work of Alcuin has the same aim and value, though at a level far lower even than the garbled pseudo-classical knowledge of the 6th century.

Alcuin himself was the product of the Irish and Northumbrian monastic traditions. Since the 5th century, a highly developed culture of its own type had existed in the monasteries of Kells and Durrow, as seen in a rich verbal literature and in the superb illuminations of the "Book of Kells". Beside this, the Irish monks were pioneers in the approach to Classical study, copying grammars and compiling word-lists. Anglo-Saxon monks of the 7th and 8th centuries took up the Irish tradition, first based on York and the north, then on Canterbury. Bede of Jarrow, Egbert of York, were pioneers in this educational work, and it fell to Egbert's pupil Alcuin (735–804) to establish the far-reaching reforms at Charlemagne's Palace School which were to provide a permanent basis of medieval education. His first aim was to establish a standard of correct spelling throughout the Empire. He also developed the Carolingian minuscule script, in which were written some of the finest manuscripts of the Middle Ages. Charlemagne's legislation gave effect to Alcuin's plans for schools associated with monasteries and cathedrals. Laymen could be admitted, but the education was primarily designed to give training for the priesthood. From these cathedral schools the future universities were to spring. In designing their curricula, Alcuin adopted the *trivium* and *quadrivium* and planned their use for the understanding of scripture. (The application of music, as a subject of the *quadrivium* was to the knowledge of plainsong and to Boethius' account of Greek theory.)

The work of Alcuin and Charlemagne cannot be regarded as an early Renaissance; it was simply a first step in elementary education. Even so, it barely survived in the century following the death of Charlemagne in 814, which witnessed the break-up of the Frankish empire, the persistent pressure of Slavs and Saracens, and the added onslaughts of fierce and destructive Norsemen. The Ottonian dynasty, taking its name from the kings who succeeded in holding the eastern boundaries of Europe, could contribute little beyond this defensive function, and the destructive raids of the Vikings nearly brought down the whole structure of organized life in the West.

It is in the arts that the European character begins to reveal itself during these formative years. Even here, the appearance of individual works of high achievement should not distort our perspective. Artistic impulse was clearly present; it always is in any age. But a stable environment for its full and consistent flowering did not exist, except for a time in the period of Charlemagne, and our main interest lies in observing the reaction of the northern races to the cross-currents of different traditions which they inherited.

First, in the visual arts. The products of their native tradition, like all nomadic art, depend on decoration and design applied to portable objects for domestic and military use, or for personal adornment. Interpenetration of earlier Scythian and Celtic styles had brought into being a highly complex art, using interlacing and spiral patterns, rows of circles and wave-bands, framed within border-strips which might employ either geometrical or animal figuration. This is an art—unlike that of the Mediterranean— hardly concerned at all with representation of the human figure. A distinctive artistic temperament is revealed, and when it is brought to play upon the religious subject-matter of Christianity, we meet some fruits of the nascent European genius which have high value in themselves as well as pointing ahead to features of medieval art. The great technical skill and fantastic imagination of the Celtic miniaturists appears in the "Book of Kells", probably dating from the 9th century. Plate 4 shows features of that ancient calligraphic art, allied with Christian symbolism, in one of the most famous of illuminated manuscripts.

A more practical application of art to religious purposes was not overlooked in Charlemagne's schemes of education. Einhard, a pupil of Alcuin, was in charge of the Palace workshops, in which the Carolingian tradition of art was created. His aim was didactic; the first duty of the artist should be to tell his story as clearly as possible. In Charlemagne's words: "Painting is admissible in churches, in order that those who are unlettered may yet read by gazing at the walls what they cannot read in books." The Franks had decorative skill, but they had to learn how to visualize a scene. Einhard, being an admirer of the antique style, turned to Classical models, which were available in the book-paintings, ivory-carvings, jewel- and metal-work, brought by traders, pilgrims, and royal personages. In this way, forms and subject-matter as conceived by ancient Christian artists provided the basis for a new didactic art. The Roman traditions of narrative style and portrayal of single figures—more assimilable than the ecstasies of Byzantine art—passed into European culture in the form of Bible stories, lives of saints, portraits of psalmists and evangelists, and of Christ himself, with attributes of worldly rather than heavenly triumph. The vivid line-drawings illus-trating the Utrecht Psalter (c. 800) show the reactions to narrative style of a particularly lively school of artists based on Rheims. Another 9th-century work (Plate 2), one of a pair of ivory panels representing an archbishop surrounded by singing deacons, is more than a portrait; it is a symbolic representation of the liturgy itself. In this respect it draws attention to the allegorical character which is such a conspicuous feature of medieval art. More still, it reminds us that perspective and exact representation of nature play very little part in pre-Renaissance European art. The figures here are unrelated in size and position to their back-ground, and show that the artist is concerned with the image presented to the mind, not to the physical eye. The search for the "real", behind physical reality, is a characteristic of art which is called "primitive", whether in the past or in the 20th century.

Charlemagne spoke of wall-paintings in churches. Very little of Carolingian architecture survives, except in small, remote churches which have not undergone rebuilding. Several Saxon examples such as Brixworth, Earl's Barton, St. Martin (Canter-bury), and Escomb (Durham), remain in England and show the plain and solid style. The chapel which was built by Charlemagne at Aachen between 796 and 804 (destroyed and rebuilt in the following century) owed its plan to the octagonal shape of S. Vitale, Ravenna, but it showed in the massive plainness of its piers that it was created by men who were utterly incapable of realizing the mystery and subtlety of its ancient prototype. Another church with historical associations, S. Ambrogio, Milan, was founded in the 4th century by St. Ambrose, raised on its present plan in 850, and rebuilt with vault and dome in the

12th century. The famous Benedictine monastery of St. Gall (about 820) is one of a large number of similar foundations which spread over Europe and became the homes of such tranquil and cultivated life as could be maintained in this ungracious era. They provided the environment for monastic life, and formed the basis of the great Romanesque architecture which was to rise in the 11th century.

The part played by monasticism in medieval life is widely acknowledged. In music, its influence was paramount. The self-contained communities which spread over Europe from the 6th century onward, although founded on the conception of religious dedication, were centres for all the activities of life, practical and artistic as well as religious. It is important to distinguish the purely devotional impulse from the human ones which must arise in such all-embracing communities. The existence of many different occupations led naturally to specialization and to the cultivation of professional skills. The urge to artistic creation acted with great force in music, because monastic life was centred on the celebration of the services of the Hours and the Mass, and the vehicle for this worship was plainsong. This music of Oriental nature and origin is supremely fitted for association with the moods of religious worship. St. Augustine was not alone in responding to the ecstasies it induces. Its closeness to pentatonic melody, which is also common in folk-song, betoken its "primitive" appeal and its nearness to the roots of human nature. Its origin in incantation, the hypnotic suggestion arising from its antiphonal recitation, its avoidance of the rhythms of ordinary life, its place in a ritual of strongly sensuous appeal—these are potent influences on the nature of men living a cloistered life. The consciously intellectual part of the mind is least active in this musical atmosphere; the human will is least assertive and the worshipper is the more submissive to the higher power to whom his thoughts are directed. There could be no more appropriate musical counterpart to the life of prayer. It is not surprising that the greatest era of plainsong composition, from the 5th to the 8th centuries, coincided with the period when monastic life required its constant use. Here was the maturing of an ancient art under conditions which favoured a concentrated employment of its resources.

There is no doubt that sheer delight in music played its part in this flowering of ecclesiastical melody. Plainsong fulfilled the needs of worship, but it also provided an outlet for artistic expression. In the early 9th century the art of church singing was so assiduously cultivated as to provoke clerical complaints that singers were neglecting their spiritual education. Throughout its history, the Church, whilst maintaining the Christian doctrine and ensuring its appropriate expression in art, had to reckon with the irrepressible individuality of the European peoples. Written records cannot show the balance of forces in this struggle, since secular music was either improvised or handed down by tradition. The old *scop* and *gleeman*, known from the 9th century as *jongleur*, provided the entertainment and narrated the exploits of the northern races, and from the 10th century the *goliards*, on the fringe of the ecclesiastical world, added their quota of ribaldry and satire. As long as the Church dominated European life and thought, the stream of secular art continued, apparently, to be a secondary one. In actual life, at all periods, it must have occupied a far larger place than appears from the written record. More important than the incorporation of pagan feasts and secular melody into ecclesiastical usage, a decided musical character is revealed as soon as examples of the popular art become available (from the 11th century in the vernaculars, a little earlier in Latin). Some of the basic features which were ultimately to distinguish the music of Europe from any other music were already present. The characteristic major scale appears early, for instance in the Latin secular song *O admirabile Veneris idolum*, perhaps of the 10th century, and continues in song, dance, and dramatic entertainment through centuries of ecclesiastical modal preoccupation. It is easy to attribute something of a chordal sense to much of this popular melody, and the regular use of stringed instruments which could be thrummed would accentuate any leanings towards texture in depth as distinct from purely melodic declamation. The tendency to regular rhythmical verse was growing (the metrical accent had long since replaced Classical scansion by quantity), and balancing phrases in pairs of verses were becoming common in both secular and ecclesiastical usage. Finally, and most significantly, the practice of simultaneous singing of melodies at different pitches, which is attributed to the northern peoples, especially in Britain, and which began to assert itself in ecclesiastical chant from the 9th century, is one which was to transform the art of music in the coming centuries. The sum of all these tendencies is momentous. Plainsong, beautiful as it is, and forming the basis of a unique artistic synthesis during the centuries of Western polyphonic art, was not destined to remain the typical music of the West. The musical genius of the Teutonic and Latin races was to develop on other lines, and long before the climax of the Middle Ages, signs of this individuality were beginning to appear.

But at the beginning of the 9th century, the immediate task of the Church was one of organization and education, in furtherance of Charlemagne's enlightened policy. Uniformity was prescribed, and chant was regulated according to the Gregorian Antiphonary. The tendency to use metre and rhyme in new chant texts, the efforts to improve the notation of music, the addition of words in simple syllabic form to some of the florid melodic passages of plainsong—these are signs of a systematic approach in educating clergy and singers. As a policy for broadening the base of the Church and its music, it could hardly fail to achieve results; as far as it was aimed to restrict the individual creative urges of its musicians, it was doomed, like all similar efforts, to failure. Insistence on the uniformity of the basic liturgy did not preclude invention at those points where optional additions (*trope* and *sequence*) could be tolerated. Similarly, short interpolations of dialogue in the Easter and Christmas stories developed, by the 11th century, into plays and music-dramas which not only satisfied the rich creative and responsive faculties of medieval people, but contributed to the ultimate development of the drama in general. The northern peoples were absorbing the Christian tradition, and doing so through the imaginative medium of art.

SUMMARY

Out of the upheaval of these centuries the Church emerged as the dominant figure. It could exert a formidable political influence, but stood far above the shifting balances of the temporal world, since it was the exponent of the Christian faith and the controller of the mind of Europe. Before the end of the ancient world it had defined its basic doctrines and preserved a tenuous thread of Classical knowledge, edited for the safe use of the faithful. This was the mental face of Europe. Charlemagne's contribution was to provide an organization within which barbarous people could learn enough language to absorb it. The only glow of creative life in the period came from the arts. The northern genius developed its own tradition in some exquisite decorative art, and, in learning from ancient models the forms in which Christianity could be interpreted, it began to reveal its own potentiality in spiritual expression. In music, the essentially religious art of plainsong reached its finest expression in the Christian ritual which was the life-blood of the Church. In that unselfconscious identification with the life of prayer it retained its artistic purity, but before the year 1000, professional cultivation and racial instinct had already started a process of transformation which was to last through five centuries of musical history.

4

The Climax of the Middle Ages

1000–1300

By the year 1000 relative peace had succeeded the invasions, populations and trade were in a phase of growth which was to last until the 14th century, cultivated land was replacing woods and marshes, villages growing into walled towns, great fairs becoming famous on the trade routes, and tribal life giving way to more broadly based and settled ways of life in geographical if not national states. A new life was quickening among the peoples of Europe and a momentum beginning which was to carry them forward to a unique phase of their civilization in the 13th century.

The word Christendom has a familiar ring. It brings to our mind, as much as one word can, the composite picture of ecclesiastical, feudal, and burgher society which we associate with the Middle Ages. It was in fact the term currently used before the idea of Europe as a geographical entity became established. It serves to emphasize the dominant rôle of Christianity in the medieval world, but it should not be taken to imply any unanimity of thought or conduct, but rather a synthesis of many disparate elements, a compromise which existed, often uneasily, between Church and State, and also within the Church itself. To understand the Western mind in general it is essential to observe the interplay of forces in this particular age both for the civilization they produced in their own time and for the reactions they provoked throughout subsequent history. It was primarily an "age of faith", but it produced intellectual as well as spiritual achievements by many great minds which were searching for the principles which govern the relation of man to the forces greater than man. The following sentences from R. R. Bolgar's *The Classical Heritage* give the exact perspective: "The civil power was stronger than it had been in the Dark Ages, but it was not yet strong enough to stand alone; and in any case men were not accustomed to look elsewhere than to the Church for support. So at this time the loss of religious faith was still looked upon as a social danger.... The world of Aquinas had what the world of Erasmus was to lack—an overwhelming desire to retain the Christian pattern of life."

What reason was there to fear the loss of religious faith? Economic and social changes had brought about new educational and intellectual requirements. The needs of practical life called for fuller knowledge of law, medicine, and science, and the source of information was in the writings of the ancients. Legal study had preserved some continuity in Italy since Roman times, but a new access to Classical knowledge was now available through contact with Arabian civilization. Islam, like Christianity, had turned to Greek philosophy in shaping its religious thought, and its scholars were able to pass on through their translations new aspects of Aristotle's logic, and wider ranges of medical and scientific knowledge than had hitherto been accessible to Europe. Both religions found increasingly the need to reconcile the conflicting claims of faith and reason. In the Christian church, closer study of the writings of the Fathers and of the Old Testament revealed contradictions which were disturbing to many minds. As the new logical method became available, it was eagerly adopted as a means to explain, or explain away, these discrepancies. Already in the 11th century, Berengar of Tours showed the new outlook in claiming that all truth could be examined in the light of reason. This attitude—duly condemned by the Church in 1050—was diametrically opposed to the orthodox position, which still rested on the thought of St. Augustine. This was that knowledge can only come by belief, and only those possessing God's grace can want to believe and therefore come to know. The extreme Augustinian dependence on belief alone could not be expected to satisfy minds which were rapidly assimilating new habits and methods of reasoning. Dialectic dominated the thought of the 11th century and was its foundation in the 12th, whether in argument for or against the claims of reason. Anselm (1033–1109) was the first to apply it as an aid to belief. Abelard (1079–1142) furthered the use of rational argument in support of faith by his critical approach to the meaning of words and concepts. Peter Lombard, teaching at the Cathedral School of Paris from 1140 to 1160 produced in his *Sentences* a standard medieval textbook which resolved the contradictory statements of the Church Fathers by means of dialectic, and contributed to the technical method of 13th-century scholasticism. St. Thomas Aquinas (1226–74) brought to a culmination these two centuries of effort in the application of reason to revelation, in his *Summa against the Gentiles* and his *Summa Theologica*, in which he achieved a reconciliation of Aristotelian logic and sensory knowledge with Christian belief. He recognized the senses as the source of all human knowledge, but the findings of human reason and experience must give way if they come into conflict with the dictates of faith. For the theologian, this must be so, since he is not following reason for its own sake but in order to support certain assumptions. Unlike the pure philosopher, he can accept the validity of revealed truth.

Aquinas's doctrine became the official one of the Church after she had shown some initial nervousness about dependence on the pagan Aristotle. The Church's suspicion was justified by developments which were taking place in the Universities. The oldest of these institutions, Salerno and Bologna, were practical in their emphasis on law and medicine, and non-ecclesiastical in character. Not so Paris, which was founded in 1200 and closely connected with the Church from the beginning. Every student had to pass through the Arts faculty and acquire a grounding in the main branches of profane knowledge before proceeding to other study. Since Aristotle's books provided the materials of this course, a wide range of subjects including ethics and all the physical sciences was covered, and there was an increasing tendency to pursue learning for its own sake and not merely as a preparation for theological study. Dependent as the Arts course was on Aristotle it could constitute a rival system of thought to that of the Church.

The danger to Christian theology lay not only in the actual work of Aristotle but in the commentaries of the Arabian philosophers who had transmitted his works. The most significant to the Western mind was Averroes (1126–78), whose aim, like that of Aquinas, was to reconcile the claims of faith and reason; unlike Aquinas he refused to admit the supremacy of faith. Of the philosophers who had transmitted his works. The most significant the most prominent was Siger of Brabant (1240–84). He held views which led logically to the denial of personal immortality and other dogma of the Church. He, like Averroes, was obliged to think of faith and reason as two different truths, and he was ready to follow where reason led even if it did not conform to revelation. His propositions were condemned in 1270. Heterodox philosophy however was gaining ground and it provoked churchmen like Bonaventura, Aquinas, and Albertus Magnus to controversy in defence of the faith. A second Condemnation, in 1277, was more sweeping than the first and had the effect of defining the orthodox position. The central task of the defenders of the faith was to preserve the authority of supernatural truth, and to resist the widespread belief in astral determinism, which had developed from Arabian astrology.

At this point, the Church's intellectual position was still secure in most men's minds and the full implications of the use of reason were not yet realized. The faith moreover did not depend on intellectual expression alone. Mysticism, a search for oneness with God in spiritual communion, made a natural appeal to many, both men and women, as a reaction against the dialectic spirit so prevalent in the Middle Ages. Bernard of Clairvaux in the early 12th century had condemned Peter Abelard's reasonings as degrading the faith; the Abbey of St. Victor produced a succession of mystics, and their influence culminated in the work of St. Bonaventura (1221–74), who represented the opposite pole to St. Aquinas in insisting on revealed truth and the mystical approach to God. A religion of the heart is always likely to commend itself to more people than one of the mind, and in the 12th and 13th centuries an unworldly simplicity seemed particularly desirable as a corrective to excessive intellectualism.

More desirable still was the need of a corrective to the scandalous ways of life of many of the clergy. Here we meet another cross-current of this complicated age. There is no need to labour the contrast between calling and conduct, or between the fine minds and personalities which stand out against a background of self-indulgence and ignorance. "Calling" in fact is not the word to use about the medieval clergy in general. To those not possessing land, the Church was the only avenue for advancement, or for the exercise of professional skills, or the avoidance of menial labour. Very few were "called of God", and we should not confuse a professional occupation with a profession of faith. What we are observing in the medieval church is a vast organization which had grown from what must be, in the last resort, a personal impulse—the individual's desire to establish a relationship with God. As an institution the Church was now concerned with far more than this personal religion, and was inevitably subject to the tendency of organized institutions to become the grave of the ideals to which they are dedicated. The wonder is not that human failure occurred so widely but that the Church had for so long succeeded in imposing an ideal on men of assertive individuality. That she did bring them within her civilizing orbit is our permanent gain; if they had not passed out of that tutelage to a wider world of human experience it would have been our permanent loss. In these very centuries when the Church was at the height of her spiritual and temporal power, the signs were becoming increasingly clear that she was making an impossible demand on man in centring his thought on the next world at the cost of a full life in this one. Even in monastic life, where conditions might be thought especially favourable to a life of withdrawal, the record was one of inevitable decline from unrealizable ideals. Within a century of the founding of Cluny in 909, the new order of Cistercians were speaking scathingly of its worldly splendour; it was not long before the reformed Cluniacs could return the criticism. The Dominicans and Franciscans from the early 13th century made their great contributions to religious thought and art, but their successors, as wandering friars, were to become for the most part a plague of disreputable vagabonds over the length and breadth of Europe.

Such were some of the tensions within the medieval Church. In our survey of the developing mind of Europe, we must discount the inevitable human failings which belong only to their own day, and look for those thoughts and experiences which have left their permanent mark. In the theological and philosophical speculations which reached a climax in the 13th century we can see the first mature achievements of the Western intellect. The Roman Catholic synthesis was virtually complete, and it remains as one of the many great attempts of man to reconcile the absolute and the individual, the eternal and the temporal. The life of St. Francis of Assisi (1181–1226) presents another aspect of character, one for which it would be hard to find a parallel in other civilizations. "Sell all that thou hast and give to the poor" was the conception of Jesus of Nazareth, but St. Francis provided an example of its practical application, and his memory has continued to shine brightly in the Western mind. It has borne fruit in the sense of mission shown by outstanding individuals like Florence Nightingale, and many Christian missionaries. Saints are rare, and those with the particular gifts and temperament of Francis of Assisi are rarest of all. They are a symbol of the quality of love which was the central message of Jesus, and one of the chief contributions of Christianity to the European character. Without this message, and its outstanding exemplars, our public and private ideals would not be what they are. This is not to say they are consciously based on either Christianity or on the example of Francis. We can only claim that the European character owes something it would otherwise not possess to those softening influences.

Whatever gifts of mind and character posterity may owe to Christianity, the glories of medieval architecture bear witness to the powerful hold which the Church then had on the contemporary mind. The monasteries had already provided the stimulus, and the means, for massive building in the later years of the Dark Ages. The reform movement spreading from Cluny in the 10th century covered Europe with "a white robe of churches", which retained the traditional basilican form and rounded arches of the early Church, and so gave the name Romanesque to the style which they heralded. (Plate 5.) But they also revealed features which made this style the first distinctively European contribution to architecture. Some of these arose directly from the needs of the Church. The growing worship of saints called for additional chapels and altars which began to appear in clusters around the apse, or at the eastern ends of the aisles. Christian symbolism, as well as practical need, led to the adoption of the cruciform plan, in which transepts were added and a lengthened chancel replaced the ancient apse. Christian insistence too on aspiration to a world higher than the physical one led naturally to an architecture which emphasizes upward, soaring lines. The addition of towers and spires, and in Italy the appearance of the separate bell-tower or campanile, are signs of a realistic interpretation of this Christian ideal. Vertical and pointed features are the hall-mark of the Gothic style, which reached its purest and most exalted expression in the 13th century. They became increasingly incorporated into the main structure of the building itself, and the key to this development is found in the evolution of stone vaulting which began, in the early 12th century, to replace the flat or domed roofs of antiquity. The Romans had solved their roofing problems by using concrete barrel-vaults supported by massive walls. The step from the heavy Romanesque style to the lofty and airy Gothic structures, with their ample window spaces, was taken when the medieval architects discovered and mastered the art of rib and panel vaulting. The principle of balance superseded that of mass, and the system found its completion in the flying-buttresses and superimposed pinnacles which countered the outward stresses of the vaulting ribs. (Plate 6.)

Romanesque architecture owed its origin and development to monastic inspiration. The Gothic phase, which lasted from about 1150 to 1350 in its purest form, had a wider basis and appeal. This was the period of secular cathedrals and churches, that is, those ministering to the whole community, not just to cloistered monks. It was the age too of the new cities, or communes, which had grown rich through trade. The general mood of the 13th century was one of joyous confidence, and of freedom and expansion. Vigorous communities of widely differing types sought corporate expression, and the only unifying ideal was that of Christianity. The new cathedrals and churches were the visible symbols of this ideal. It would be quite mistaken to interpret the artistic creations of this age as primarily an expression of religious fervour. They were the result of a corporate exaltation of spirit, deriving from many sources but expressible only in terms of the one prevailing belief. It is obvious too that architectural achievements of the supreme order of those of the 13th century depended on highly developed professional knowledge and skill, and on the genius of individual architects and sculptors. The fully independent artist and craftsman have emerged, and their works can be enjoyed for their own sake as art, and not just as adjuncts of worship.

The sculpture of the 13th century shows most clearly the scaling of a summit in pure art. In the first part of the century Christian symbolism prevailed over human expression, in stiff attitudes and draperies, and in the idealization of faces. Within a short span of years a vitalizing of forms was apparent. The great doorways of Amiens, Rheims, Laon, and Notre-Dame de Paris show the sculptors keeping a perfect balance between the portrayal of real human beings and their placing in an architectural environment. (See Plates 7 and 8.) Within a few years again, in the early 14th century, this interest in human expression was to be carried to undue lengths in the creation of arresting figures, emphatic gestures and exaggerated shadows which disturb the architectural lines and overstep the conventions of this particular form of art.

Thirteenth-century architecture and sculpture invited appreciation as purely artistic creations, quite apart from their religious associations. It is not so with the other arts. Painting, as a Western creation, was not yet in being; the rigid symbolism of

Byzantine art still prevailed in church decoration and so did the Germanic tradition of intimate and often fascinatingly grotesque illumination of manuscripts. Drama was in its embryonic stage. As an expression of the popular imagination it played a growing and indeed intense part in medieval life, in the form of Mystery, Miracle and Morality Plays, now rapidly developing from their original form of interpolations in the liturgy. Increasing emphasis on comic by-play and shrewd observation of character encouraged secular tendencies. By the early 14th century the venue was out-side the church, and townsfolk and guilds of players replaced the clergy as actors. A three-hundred-year process of development was to culminate in the great cycles of the 15th century. Already before 1200, a large-scale drama, *Adam*, partly in Anglo-Norman, partly in Latin, had shown the qualities of realism in action, and subtlety in satire and observation which are features of popular art. The first appearance of the Faust theme is seen in Ruteboef's *Le Miracle de St. Théophile* (c. 1284). In these cycles of Mysteries and Moralities, there begins an exploration of the deeper issues of life, with which we are familiar in subsequent European tragic drama. In their earlier stages, they are dealing with these subjects in the manner of a folk-art, parallel to that of music in the sublimation of human experience in folk-song.

What is the position of music (as a cultivated art) in this period? It was widely prevalent as a vehicle for both religious and secular expression and had its fully professional exponents, indeed its men of genius, who now definitely emerge from anonymity. In many respects, Gregorian chant provided the foundation of the art, both within and without the church, and developments on that traditional basis had taken a decisive shape before the close of the 13th century. They had not yet culminated in a musical language which an average listener of post-medieval times would recognize as his own, or appreciate without historical interpretation. This is not to belittle the efforts of that age. We can pay tribute to the accomplishments of its musicians more justly if we regard them as vitally constructive contributions to a process of development far outspanning any single generation, than by making sweeping comparisons with the fully matured art of contemporary architecture or sculpture. The 13th century was indeed one of the greatest in European history, but not by any means only for its finished achievements.

A brief outline of the evolution of church music will make this clear. Before the close of the Dark Ages the habit had developed of reinforcing the single line of plainsong by simultaneous singing at a different pitch. At first this was simply a parallel movement of voices at the fixed interval of a fourth or a fifth. By the 11th century a more varied interplay of the voices was recognized (one voice could rise while the other fell), more intervals were available, and by the end of that century quicker notes in an upper voice were being sung against slower ones in the voice chanting the plainsong. Here already is the defining characteristic of European music: the idea of playing or singing together melodies which have a separate individuality. The term "polyphony" (multiple sound) is generally applied to this art of combined singing, which was developed first on the basis of actual plainsong, and later with freely composed melody which had close affinity with the contours and modal character of plainsong. This art, with its emphasis on the character of the separate voices, or "parts", reached a climax in the 16th century. Long before then, another aspect of musical texture had emerged: the blending of simultaneous sounds in "harmony" is a factor which cannot be disregarded in giving significant order to a musical texture. Taste has varied in this matter of harmony. The fourths and fifths of the 9th and 10th centuries, the common chord which began to establish itself as a standard of reference in the 15th century, and the untrammelled combinations of the 20th century are examples of this variability.

The three elements which are indispensable in the European conception of concerted music are therefore melody, rhythm (the organization of sounds in time), and harmony. In the period covered by this chapter the decisive steps were taken which transformed an art of non-metrical solo chanting into the complex and measured textures with which we are now familiar. The controlling factor in the process was rhythm. Two or more people performing different melodies together must have a method of synchronizing, and of conforming to their chosen convention of harmony. Between 1150 and 1250 the method of composing was to break the chant up into sections, lengthen each of its notes, and add two melodies which preserved their own independence. Six rhythmic modes, or patterns equivalent to poetic metres, imposed rigidity which was only gradually relaxed as more flexible rhythmical organization was achieved in the measured music of the "Ars Nova" in the 14th century. At all prominent points, such as the beginning and end of phrases, and at each metrical accent, the traditional concords—octaves, fourths, and

4. A page from the Book of Kells, probably 9th century. St. Matthew.
(Trinity College, Dublin.)

5. Laach Abbey Church, Rhineland. 1156.

6. Notre Dame de Paris. 1163–1235.

fifths—were used. Between those points, discord was ignored and melodies were given their freedom.

The European urge towards construction and complexity here makes its first impact on music. Racial character also appears in the original melodies added to the basic plainsong fragments. The secular element is strong, and the preoccupation with rhythm brings the dance and the popular song to mind. In fact the late 13th century motet used well-known songs of the day as material for the added voice or voices, and instruments also supported the plainsong *canto firmo*, as the basis was called. The separation of religious and secular life is a modern characteristic. The zest for life of the medieval citizen and his directly human interpretation of the Bible stories and the Church's doctrine is evident in the drama which grew out of the liturgy, and it is this quality of vitality and unselfconscious expression which gives value to the music of the period. The plainsong melody virtually lost its recognizable form in those parts of the Mass where musical elaboration was needed, and this, along with the structural innovations, was a notable step in the assertion of European musical character.

A still more significant expression of this character is found in the secular music of the period, not only of the popular kind with its ever-present dance rhythms, but in the recherché art of the Troubadours. This feature is a structural one, and it derives from the forms of lyric poetry which were now taking shape in the vernacular languages. These forms themselves owed much to popular and traditional dance-steps, since troubadours worked in partnership with minstrels, and their rhythms and phrases had often to be suitable for performance by voice and fiddle in accompaniment to a dance. Regular metre, balancing phrases, verses and sections, rhymes, and refrains—elements which were fully established in poetic practice by the end of the 13th century —are also elements of musical structure. Poetry and music were indivisible in the elaborate courtly art of the 12th and 13th centuries, an art which spread widely throughout Europe from its original Provençal source. In doing so it gave currency to forms like the *ballade*, *virelai*, and *rondeau*, which enjoyed long popularity in their own age. But more than that, it emphasized the European tendency towards symmetrical musical structure and away from the unmeasured declamation of plainsong. In this respect, the secular art of the 12th and 13th centuries made its contribution not only to the rich life of that age but to the typically European conception of music which was developing its modes of expression. We see music once more in its two aspects: as a part of contemporary life, and at a stage of its technical evolution.

This second aspect involves reference to features which are important in understanding the language of music. Individual forms and works are far too numerous even to be listed in this brief survey, but there is an ample literature both of recorded sound and of the written word through which the Middle Ages can live again in our mind. The picture which emerges is that of a virile native music asserting itself independently of the ancient ecclesiastical tradition which had hitherto monopolized cultivated art. Although much Troubadour melody bears the imprint of Gregorian chant, there is much that is purely European both in the structural symmetries which have been mentioned and in the use of the major scale. But above all, it is in the expressive nature of this art that we perceive a new development in Western experience. The subjects which concern the poet and musician as a human being were taking the place of those devoted to religious worship. A new range of feeling was opening up, and since solo melody was free from the polyphonic problems which confronted the church composers, these newly liberated feelings could find spontaneous expression.

The art of the troubadours and trouvères, and their successors the Minnesingers, was mainly centred on the prevailing theme of Courtly Love, an artificial convention of the knight's fealty to his lady, an idealization of sexual love outside marriage. It was an art of courts, although it had its counterpart at humbler levels, where the same universal theme was treated with all shades of meaning, from the wit and ribaldry of the townsfolk of France to the sober intensity of their German neighbours. Another new theme came into the experience of the West in the 12th century— that of heroism. It was new, at any rate, in our literature, although as ancient as the races themselves in song and narration. Even when the *Chansons de Geste*, the epics of warlike deeds, appeared in written form, they were still not designed for reading, but for recitation to a simple musical formula, endlessly repeated by the jongleurs. The *Chanson de Roland*, the stories of *Guillaume Cournez Count of Orange*, the *Cid*, the Arthurian legends and the quest of the Grail, the Norse Sagas, the Germanic legends of *Siegfried* and the *Nibelungen*—these legendary figures form a tapestry in the background of our thought. Even if we

have not met them in their original form, they have come to life
in the imaginative re-creations of subsequent literature. Time
and distance have softened some of their violence and brutality,
and their authors moreover are not simply recounters of exploits.
They are clearly concerned with moral issues of courage, loyalty,
freedom, and justice. Our own Beowulf, in a far earlier age, had
shown the true heroic temper in accounting for his success: "By
my right hand and by the help of God". Again, in the *Chanson
de Roland*, the issue is not simply one of heroism; it is complicated by the human failing of pride. Roland could have saved
himself and his companions by blowing his horn for help.

A probing of the more subtle qualities of mind appears in the
Romances which followed the Epics. *Aucassin et Nicolette* (about
1230), a love-story with a happy ending, is exceptional in not
conforming to the convention of courtly love, and in reversing
the normal view of the respective attractions of heaven and hell.
More in line with the thought of its day was the *Roman de la
Rose*, also about 1230 in its first conception by Guillaume de
Lorris, but completed about forty years later by the more cynical
Jean de Meun. This allegorical romance, exercising a fascination
in its day and a literary influence long outlasting the Middle
Ages, brings into highlight some distinctive traits of mind and
imagination. It did not initiate them, but it presented them with
the illumination that only art can give. The first is the psychological approach to human understanding and conduct. Professor
C. S. Lewis, in *The Allegory of Love*, refers to a new attitude to
moral questions which developed in the centuries when Christianity was emerging, the idea of conflict between good and evil.
This conception, that different qualities exist within the same
individual, led easily to the idea of personifying them and showing their interaction in allegorical form. A second distinctive trait
emerges when this allegorical method, kept alive throughout the
Dark Ages, was applied to the theme of Courtly Love in Chrétien
de Troye's *Lancelot* in the late 12th century. That author's
Tristan and Iseult has not survived, but the legend has never
failed since those medieval days to provide opportunity for exploring the human heart. If we add to this double stream of
allegory and Courtly Love the poetic search for another world,
not the "other world" of religion but the one of the imagination,
we shall come near to appreciating what Guillaume de Lorris's
Roman de la Rose brought to a focus, and what an inspiration
it gave for further poetic expression of the human spirit. The

subtle and intimate qualities of the individual became valid objects of thought, set over against the abstractions which are the counters of religious and philosophical speculation. Nor were the foibles of mankind left unobserved in this vitally human age: the *isopet* (named after Aesop) and the *fabliau*—the most famous being the racy *Roman de Renard*—provided the medium for the expression of middle-class satire, quick-wittedness, and broad humour. The art of literature came to a glorious flowering almost as the vernacular languages were putting forth their earliest branches.

The mind of Europe is the theme of this book, and persons and events must receive scant notice except for their direct contribution to the main streams of thought. But we cannot leave the 13th century without a reference to some of its striking personalities, who stand out as summits in their respective spheres, and to events like the Crusades, the emergence of cities, and of the institution of parliamentary government in England. The Crusades, inspired at first by the Christian ideal, degenerated into barbarous excursions of feudal knighthood, but they broadened the European mind through contact with new scenes, peoples, cultures, and commerce. The cities of France, Flanders, and Germany had given a new dimension to society before 1200; the People now counted as the "Third Estate" along with the Church and the nobles, and the city states of Italy were about to play their decisive part in a new phase of our civilization. There was an upsurge of confidence and vitality which has not been equalled in any other age, and a positive charge running through the society of Europe which was at its most intense concentration in figures like Innocent III, who typified the power motive dominating the papacy; and in the astonishing Frederick II, whose dazzling reign in Sicily was the marvel of the age and a nightmare to the pious. Such men of power and action held the centre of the stage in contemporary life; two other figures whom we have already met, Francis of Assisi and Thomas Aquinas, played less prominent rôles while they lived, but the power of their mind and character has left an imprint long outlasting that of the more assertive practical men of the day.

In summary, the age was one of synthesis, well expressed in the concept "Christendom". In spite of questionings by philosophers, bourgeois satire on clerical abuses, vigorous anti-papal reactions by emperor and kings, the Church still kept its hold on the general mind. It was the symbol of spiritual power, and the papacy wielded a formidable temporal power. The Catholic faith found its authoritative definition, and also a new human interpretation through St. Francis and the growing worship of the Virgin Mary. The external expression of this ecclesiastical power is seen at its greatest in Gothic architecture, sculpture, stained glass, and decorative carving. At the same time, the character of the European people revealed itself not only in the enterprise which raised finely balanced structures to unprecedented heights, in the intricacy of detail, complexity of design, and picturesque grouping, but in the scenes of their daily life and the grotesques of their own imaginative creation which are a permanent record in sculpture and decoration of the medieval synthesis of many diverse elements. This frank acceptance of life with all its incongruous juxtapositions appeared too in the popular drama which was taking shape in these centuries, and to some extent also in secular intrusions into the Church's music. The latter art was passing through a stage of technical development, while showing every sign of enthusiastic cultivation. It lived more spontaneously in the spring-like lyricism of the troubadours. The art of music conveys a feeling of youth; it does not yet pretend to deal with the issues which were the great ones of the day. These were the moral ones treated with such power of mind by philosophers, with spiritual intuition by mystics, and with poetic imagination on the broader front where all human experience was becoming the subject-matter of the vernacular literature.

5

Old and New

1300–1450

FOR a thousand years, since Constantine recognized Christianity in the early 4th century, the Church and the feudal system had been twin pillars of European society. Life had revolved about monastery and castle, and even when the great towns and churches of the High Middle Ages had changed the outward appearance of Europe and the vital energies of its peoples had found expression in a multitude of new forms, the ancient framework was stable enough to contain what was new, and old allegiances were strong enough to ensure compromise where thoughts diverged. Medieval civilization owed its character and conventions to belief in this immutable order, this conception of hierarchies both spiritual and secular which were fixed, right, and eternal. From this conviction sprang much of the violence, cruelty, and injustice which marked the age. From it, too, derived the distinctive features of the art into which beliefs were distilled: the interest in abstract qualities rather than the direct observation of human features; the placing of virtues and sins in categories fixed in texts and visual symbols; the use of allegory, Dante's *Divine Comedy* being the supreme example, living for ever through its range of imagination but applied with extraordinary precision to the interpretation of Catholic belief. This crystallizing of ideas and valuing them only in their relation with the Absolute was a necessary stage in the education of barbarous races. "The soul of the Middle Ages, ferocious and passionate, could only be led by placing far too high the ideals towards which its aspirations should tend. Thus acted the Church, thus also feudal thought." (Huizinga, *The Waning of the Middle Ages*, 1924.) But this inflexible directing of thought to another world could not serve as a permanent guide to conduct. Huizinga quotes, as an example of its incongruity, a debate in the University of Paris on the advisability of levying fees for intermediate degrees. Discussion did not touch on practical considerations at

54

all, but was based on the text "Cupidity is the root of all evil". The proposal was deemed to be heretical and contrary to divine law.

The medieval attitude was to survive, especially outside Italy, until the end of the 15th century. It did so, often with active force, and often in faded and external forms. In the evolution of the European mind it was a phase which had to exist, but no less had to pass. The Catholic position, both spiritual and temporal, came under attacks which reduced its power and prestige. But these were external events, and were secondary to the main cause of its decline, which lay in its misdirection of human thought and belief, its placing of man in a straitjacket which distorted his natural growth. Man was no longer willing to be denied his fulfilment in the present world, and he was seeking a belief which could spring from his own convictions and develop his own personal responsibility. European man was beginning to explore ranges of thought and experience which gave new dimension to his mind. In his quest he could include religious experience, but his moral outlook must be determined with his own acquiescence and not instilled in him by the fear of hell.

The spirit which prompted this quest was that which characterized the Renaissance. The conception is familiar—a rebirth of the "whole man", particularly as understood in antiquity, after his partial eclipse by barbarism and medieval theology. (The idea is confused by the application of the term "Humanism" to the revival of Classical literature and its enthusiastic cultivation from the 14th century onwards.) It would be as futile to attribute dates as to attempt any precise definition of Renaissance. It is enough to describe it as an attitude of mind which by its emphasis on man and the present is sharply differentiated from that of the Middle Ages with its emphasis on God and the hereafter. Until the 16th century the two attitudes could be found in Europe, often in startling contrast, but sometimes shading into one another. Indeed, throughout the Middle Ages, although feudalism and the Christian world-view had dominated thought they did not completely permeate society. There was a fund of latent human energy which was neither fully absorbed nor fully expressed in the prevailing institutions of the Middle Ages. This can be sensed in the compromises of the Church with pagan festivals and popular singing and drama; in the cultivation by the more studious clergy of such Classical reading as was available; in works like the *Carmina Burana* and the *Fabliau*, which sprang from irrepressible human impulses; and in church carvings which show the medieval sculptor's zest for the life of the world around him. "The average artist would carve saints to order, but where he was free he often preferred to carve sinners." (G. G. Coulton, *Art and the Reformation*.) This assertion of human vitality below the level of the prevailing forms and ideals of an age is common to all epochs. It is certainly with us in the 20th century, and the pictures of Hogarth and Rowlandson recall its presence in an earlier and far more genteel civilization.

What was new at the opening of the 14th century was the liberation of the human spirit from subservience; the realization that individual effort could bring the rewards hitherto attributable only to noble birth and divine grace. This conviction owed much to the social attitudes developed in the competitive life of the city states of Northern Italy. Rivalry in trade and struggles for political existence had bred habits of forthright action and self-dependence. Personal achievement rather than noble birth could bring power and esteem, and with the acquiring of position went the desire for fame. Petrarch's theme of *"fama"* as the just and inevitable reward of *"virtus"* was a congenial one to the successful individualists of the age, one that was later to be amply developed in the splendour of Renaissance courts. For Petrarch (1304–74) and his successors, fame was the natural reward of literary success, a conception which was scarcely current before his age. Dante (1265–1321) accorded affectionate reverence to Virgil in his *Divine Comedy*, making him the image of Human Wisdom, the best that man can become in his own strength. Both these poets made an inestimable contribution to the mind of Europe in developing the power of poetic expression, and in this alone they justified the new claim of poetry to rank in the highest ranges of thought. But it is the difference between the two men which marks a turning point in thought. Dante's is still a completely medieval mind, attuned to the Christian and imperial world-order: "If the whole is right the individual is right." Petrarch also accepts the medieval idea that all truth is of The Truth, but for him, morality is not to be imposed by legislation but to be achieved by individual effort. He does not accept theological argument as a final arbiter; he searches within his own mind, and he seeks to clarify his own thought and that of his age by reference to the ideals of antiquity. His blending of the religious and humanist ideals is the key to the noblest thought of the 14th century. The rest of Europe came to look to Italy as the exemplar of this attitude. The mood was everywhere still strongly religious in spite of bitter disillusion about the state of the Church, and here was an ideal which seemed to be both noble and practicable.

In this phase of transition from one order of ideas to another the artist was feeling his way, intuitively, towards the expression of the developing mind of the community. The stage was set, in the practical world, for a glorification of individual achievement. Petrarch had the genius and the temperament to bring this mood to artistic focus. The way was not unprepared. This had been the attitude of Classical literature, of which an increasing part had become available and assimilated. Lyric poetry was the medium through which Petrarch explored the contrasting sentiments within himself, and in this art, his immediate predecessors in Italy had made significant advances beyond the artificialities which prevailed so largely in troubadour song. The old theme of unrequited love, though often present, was enriched by thoughts which arose from observed life: the gentle heart could call forth devotion as well as the rich and high-born; the subtler mixtures of bitter-sweet reflected more truly the actuality of experience. Although tricks and artifices in expression persisted, there were new developments in the poetic medium itself; the *canzone* and *sonnet* appeared as new forms, the Tuscan language flowered as the *dolce stil nuovo*, and there was an ever-increasing consciousness of purely artistic purpose. With Petrarch, lyric poetry soared above the decorative, the didactic, the entertaining, and became a communication from mind to mind not only temporal but for all time. The *Canzoniere* in which he expressed his love for Laura reveal the poet more than the lady herself. It is this self-revelation, this contemplation of the conflict between desire and reason which interests us in retrospect. It did not make its full impact in its own day, but for us it stands out clearly as the product of a new type of mind. This was the only work of Petrarch in the Italian language. The rest of his writing was in Latin, and the best part of his life was spent in travelling and observing the European scene, collecting coins and manuscripts, and arousing by his personal frendships and correspondence an enthusiasm for Classical literature. Petrarch sought in the ancient world a model of civilized life, and he had an urgent desire to translate the experiences of life into terms not of religion or philosophy but of art.

Petrarch's compatriots and immediate successors were more interested in his scholarship than in his lyric poetry, and came to share his conviction that Classical antiquity could provide the models for the kind of life they were seeking. There is more preparatory than intrinsic interest in most of the literature of 14th-century Italy, although Boccaccio's *Decameron* is a work of imagination in which old tales are given new life and characters live with intensity. His *Admeto* brought the pastoral, and the *ottava rima* stanza into the European tradition, and his verse romance, *Teseida* (adapted by Chaucer for his Knight's Tale), formed a link between the medieval romances and the epics of the Renaissance. The literature of Germany and France provided a foil to the brilliance of the Italian prelude and to the glowing affirmation of the human spirit which appeared in Chaucer at the end of the century. In Germany, the note of sincerity which the greatest of the Minnesingers, Walther von der Vogelweide, had sounded in his later reflective years, does not reappear. The courtly art of the Middle Ages deteriorated into artificialities in Heinrich von Meissen (Frauenlob), and into the pedantries of the 15th-century burghers, who under the name of Meistersingers dabbled in poetry and music. Poets like Guillaume de Machaut, Eustache Deschamps, and Charles d'Orleans were active in France, but here again they told of a world which was dying. Between the satire of Ruteboeuf in the 13th century and the real poetry of Villon, the last great figure of the Middle Ages in 15th-century France, the themes were either those of the outworn convention of courtly love, or were laments for the evils of the age, and preoccupation with death and the transience of all that is fair. To turn to the England of Chaucer (1340–1400) is to leave gloom behind and step into the springtime of the greatest of all literatures. The English language had finally replaced French, which had reigned officially since the Norman Conquest, and Chaucer himself had served his apprenticeship by mastering the verse forms and thought of French and Italian poetry. But he did not look merely to the past, through other men's eyes, but on the life around him, and that in such a way as to penetrate to permanent human qualities beneath passing and external appearance. In doing this he shows his English traits, as Shakespeare was to do two centuries later. Thus when he adapted his *Troilus and Criseyde* from Boccaccio he was not content with the Italian's sole emphasis on a passionate story. He enriched it with a new element of character by transforming the rôle of Pandarus, making him the centre of a comic strand which accompanies the tale of love, and putting into his mouth maxims and gossip which foreshadow Polonius in *Hamlet*. But in *The Canterbury Tales* he left all foreign sources behind and gave full reign to his powers of human observation. It was a simple but novel idea to think of a pilgrimage as a means of bringing together a group of people of every class and letting them each tell a story. But it added another facet to European thought: poetry was used as a study of man and manners. This appears not only in the wonderful portraits of the Prologue, but also during the telling of the stories, where each character comes to life as an individual, not merely a type. They discuss matters high and low, their thoughts taking colour from their characters. Ideas can exist as abstractions, but this most human of books shows them acquiring significance through their relation with living persons. Chaucer's pilgrims belong to the medieval scene, but they are not mere ciphers in a medieval world-order.

Abstract ideas had played a large part in the Christian world-order and its visual art in the Middle Ages. Symbols, conventional portrayals of holy figures with their proper precedence, their stereotyped gestures (see Plate 10), even their appropriate colours —these had become a form of picture-writing which conveyed the Church's message to medieval man and formed part of the ecclesiastical furnishing of his environment. In no sense could these paintings be considered as personal expressions of an artist's feelings. His place was not to add anything of himself but faithfully to reproduce the ancient formulas. This had become the tradition in the West, and the overpowering figures of Byzantine art had not softened their penetrating gaze, or come down from their aloof world of the spirit to share in the life of man in the world. But at the opening of the 14th century the work of a Florentine genius set European painting on a course which it was to follow until the 20th century. With Giotto (1266–1337) Christian art presents its message in terms of human feeling, not in a language of symbols. Such a scene as *The Deposition of Christ from the Cross*, a fresco in the Scrovegni Chapel, in Padua (Plate 9), must have revealed to its first observers a living aspect of their religion which had become overlaid with outward forms and conventions. Here, the women and disciples form a group of actual people with natural postures, dramatic gestures, and expressions which show their emotional reaction to the situation. The artist clearly had a new aim, but one which is not attributable solely to his personal genius. He was bringing to a focus in painting the urges to human expression which had grown increasingly insistent in the late 13th century. We have seen how Gothic architecture had come to its finest flowering as the expression of a corporate spirit; the more personal art of painting was now to be the medium through which a humanized religion could find an outlet.

Various factors had contributed to the growing individual emphasis in religion. The papacy, which by alliances and intrigues had broken the imperial power in the 13th century, had lost its universality and was itself reduced to being a political puppet of the French monarchy in the century which followed. While these external symbols of medieval power were visibly declining, new spiritual forces were gathering strength. The strain of mysticism was prominent, though its full effects were to be experienced later in Germany and the Netherlands. In religious philosophy, Duns Scotus (c. 1266–1308) had asserted the separate functions of faith and reason and the nobility of the human will in its search for the good. But it was Francis of Assisi who gave the most powerful impetus to private devotion and a simple religion charged with feeling. His influence was widespread, and indeed was felt by the Church to weaken the solidarity of ecclesiastical organization. It was the element of emotion which gave cogency to his appeal, and it was in this religious atmosphere that Giotto began to paint. It is significant that much of his work was devoted to illustrating scenes from the life of St. Francis. But what he received from his environment in stimulus and in spiritual outlook he transmuted into the terms of art, giving to succeeding painters a new kind of vision. Where hitherto artists had rung the changes on prescribed formulas, they were now to look into the mind and heart of their fellowmen. They were to bring to religious scenes the lively perception they had already learnt to apply to the living things of the ordinary world. The sketch below the Biblical scene from the *Queen Mary Psalter*, about 1310 (Plate 10), shows that this was not just a matter of a new technique; that had long existed. It was simply that liveliness had not been considered appropriate to religious subjects. Giotto's was a new outlook, and it brought the full range of spiritual experience within the painter's sphere. It made a powerful impression on contemporaries: Boccaccio said that Giotto's representations not only resembled but seemed to be the things themselves. This new revelation of the artist's power brought fame to Giotto in person such as had never been accorded to the traditional artist-craftsman, and more widely, it brought recognition to artists as a class. Henceforth the history of art became that of individual artists, and its value came to be enhanced in proportion as it was enriched by their personal contributions. The idea of art for its own sake could exist as well as the idea of art as a servant of religion.

At the same time, economic forces played their quiet rôle. G. G. Coulton tells us: "Popes set even distinguished sculptors to make cannon-balls, since marble, plus the time of a real artist, came cheaper in the long-run than cast-iron shot." The press-gang system also contributed: "Windsor Castle, Eton College Chapel, the Palace of Westminster, and King's College, Cambridge, were to a great extent built by pressed workmen."

Giotto was one of those "important historical figures" whose genius bears fruit not only in his own work but also in that of his successors. The new outlook and old traditions mingled in varying degrees in the art of the 14th century. Duccio preserved Byzantine forms but with softened human expression; Simone Martini maintained the emotion and active gesture of Giotto, though without his living shapes; Fra Angelico brought a new sweetness and simplicity to bear in the old two-dimensional space. The grandeur and dramatic effect of Giotto lived again in Masaccio (1401–28), but now with the added element of perspective which carried still further the conquest of reality. It was the architect Brunelleschi (1377–1446) who provided his brother painters with the mathematical basis of this new resource: with him, and with the sculptor Donatello, we enter the visual world of the Renaissance, and leave an age of transition in which the new spirit dwelt in old forms.

In the countries north of the Alps these medieval forms persisted longer than in Italy. Nevertheless they were undergoing change, and doing so in conformity with the northern character. Ecclesiastical architecture—and with this should be included the town halls, guildhalls, colleges, palaces, and bridges—showed the tendency, which was towards ever wider window-spaces filled with intricate tracery, façades crowded with sculpture, and roofs decorated with fan-vaults which no longer served a structural purpose. King's College Chapel at Cambridge is a familiar example. The balanced and soaring structures of the High Gothic gave place to wider hall-like buildings whose broad surfaces were crowded with detail almost recalling the elaboration of Celtic illuminations. In sculpture and painting too the northerners went their own way. Again it was the way of minute detail and careful representation. Jan van Eyck (1390–1441) was the central figure. He continued the tradition of the International Style which had developed in the late 14th century, and which delighted in scenes of pageantry, in costume, jewellery, animals, and flowers. The exquisite illuminations by the brothers Limburg in the Book of Hours of the Duc de Berri (1410) belong to this phase and depict the same medieval world as that of Chaucer. Van Eyck revels in the minutiae of the style, but with a closer observation of nature in his backgrounds, and with a new perception in portraiture. Succeeding northern artists followed the lead of van Eyck in method, but were content with traditional medieval themes. Lochner (1410–51) at Cologne, with his tenderly beautiful art, recalls Fra Angelico and preserves the spirit of the Middle Ages; Rogier van der Weiden (1400–64) maintains the old religious purpose with figures that might form a tableau in a mystery play. The quiet spiritual art of all these painters seems to reflect most aptly the northern temperament, especially that of the Netherlanders. With them, the medieval faith seems more tempered to humanity than in the harsher symbols which had served their predecessors. The strain was to persist, although it did not exclude a more homely and often grotesque dwelling on the practical aspects of religious faith. The new method of printing pictures by woodcuts (on the rubber-stamp principle), and then later by engraved copper plates, brought art, both pious and humorous, to a wider public, and as it contributed to the spreading of ideas over Europe, it was one of the forces which brought medieval art to an end.

Literature and painting show most clearly the direction in which thought was tending at the close of the Middle Ages. There was no widespread change, and medieval forms and attitudes persisted in many parts of Europe until well into the 15th century. In the music of the period there is little evidence of the new spirit. It was a time in which "innovations were grafted upon a basically old stock—one ending the Gothic period in music— rather than a time of broadly and essentially original creativeness". (Reese, *Music in the Middle Ages.*) One innovation which had permanent value was the rhythmical system of Proportion. In this *"Ars Nova"*, music acquired a method of controlling a wide variety of note-lenths, an advance in flexibility over the *"Ars Antiqua"* which simply knew long and short. Two fashions, rather than innovations of lasting value, were the use of *hocket* (artificial syncopation or breaking of the melody) and *isorhythm*, in which a plainsong melody arranged in a slow-moving recurring rhythmic pattern formed a thread running through the voices. The same technical methods applied to both ecclesiastical and secular music. The medieval mind was still at work here, in its own fascinating way, on the task of organizing polyphony. It was still to use it in association with words and dance, and the thought for which it was the vehicle in the 14th century belonged to the old world which was passing. This was especially so in France, where Guillaume de Machaut (1300–77) was cleric and poet and the leading composer of the day. "There never was a period in which French poetry was apparently more frail and destitute" (Prof. Legouis, *History of English Literature*), and the same author describes Machaut as "one of the most debilitated of the French poets". He may have been a better musician than poet: music has its own expressive overtones which can give significance to the flimsiest of verbal suggestions. But whether we find intrinsic interest or not in Machaut and his contemporaries, an unobtrusive process was continuing which had begun with the lyric forms of troubadour melody. The balancing phrases, rhymes, and cadences of the fixed poetic forms which were in vogue in the late Middle Ages, confirmed the tendency of European music to rhythmical regularity; and dance, carol, and folk-song continued the influence at the popular level. In this particular century also, chromatic inflexion of melody was tending to emphasize the major scale at the expense of the ecclesiastical modes. More still, the natural instinct of Italian musicians for sheer melodic beauty appeared in the later 14th century in Landini and other Florentine composers.

There could be no sharper contrast than that between the positive and creative elements in this age and its waning and decadent forms. The two ideals of Christianity and chivalry were dimmed and distorted but no others had emerged to serve the needs of a changing world. Religious belief was widely held, but the clergy were discredited and often despised; Christian thought had hardened into images and superstitions, and its message of hope had given way in too many quarters to a morbid obsession with death. Themes of decay were prevalent in sermons and in poetry; *"Ubi sunt?"*—where are the great ones of the past? "I forget his name", says Villon of one of them; or again he touches the thought with beauty in *"Où sont les neiges d'antan?"*— "Where are the snows of yester-year?" The word "macabre" was born in a poem of 1376; the Dance of Death acquired its gruesome popularity in this age, and, toying with death in the midst of life, the 15th-century Parisians held rendezvous and parties at the Churchyard of the Innocents, where skulls and bones were heaped in charnel-houses along the cloister walls for all to see. Feudal knighthood, too, had little to offer to populous communities busying themselves with industry and commerce. An episode, taken at random from the pages of Froissart's *Chronicles*—one of hundreds which he recounts as matters of daily routine—shows the decline from the ideals of chivalry. After a foray in which some prisoners had been taken but some notable ones had escaped, the revealing comment was "God! what a fortunate event it would have been, if we had taken them, for they would have paid us forty thousand francs."

Economic problems did not always assume such a simple form. Many of the practical institutions which are indispensable to our present way of life were taking shape: banking and credit systems, international commerce, large-scale as well as private industry, and even foreign travel, with Marco Polo's unprecedented sojourn of seventeen years in China. With this went the complications which are now all too familiar. The development of English cloth-weaving led in the end to a serious decline of the Flemish towns which had hitherto imported our wool. The plague of 1348, called the Black Death in England, brought not only human misery but a drastic reduction of population, with its attendant labour problems, inflated wages and prices, and the first strikes. The decade from 1375 to 1385 was one of violent unrest among both peasants and artisans, a theme which has never ceased to recur with many variations. A mobile labour force under capitalist organization emerged as a new element, and, combined with the long-established burgher class, it contributed to a broadening of the basis of society. The Third Estate exercised a political influence long before it obtained direct parliamentary representation, since with its financial and practical resources it was so useful an ally of monarchy against assertive feudal barons. By unobtrusive stages it became possible for social barriers to be crossed, and success in business and responsible public service could gain entry to a ruling class which had hitherto been recruited from those who held land and had the military strength to defend it.

As social character changed, so did the thought through which it found expression. The process of democratization took place

7. West front, Reims Cathedral. Late 13th century. The central portal.

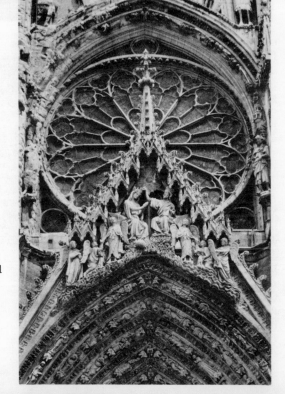

8. Reims Cathedral. The crowning of the Virgin, above the central portal.

9. (*Above*) Giotto: Deposition from the Cross. Early 14th century. Fresco in the Scrovegni Chapel, Padua.

10. The Three Magi crowned before Herod, with marginal drawing below. English, about 1310. From Queen Mary Psalter. (The British Museum, London.)

rapidly in the small successful states and towns of Italy, the Netherlands, Germany, and Switzerland. It was a far slower movement in England and France which had achieved a broader national unity in the earlier Middle Ages. The new spirit of individual human aspiration found its first outlet in the small advancing communities, and here the constructive attitude expressed itself directly in art and life. In the larger national states, the spirit of independence was no less seeking expression, but there it took the form of criticism of existing institutions, as in Langland's social complaints in *Piers Plowman*, and in Wycliffe's reactions to abuses in the Church. Starting from moral protests, he advanced by stages to a position where he placed the authority of Scripture above that of the Church. He could even attack the central mystery of the Faith, and deny the doctrine of transubstantiation. This vein of thought appealed to many serious-minded people, and being perpetuated by the Lollards in England, and Huss and his followers in Bohemia, it helped to prepare the mood in which devout people could later accept the Protestant Reformation. The influence of a notable succession of mystics, Eckhart, Suso, Tauler, and Ruysbroeck, reinforced this tendency, and gave impetus to a pietist movement called the Devotio Moderna, which left its stamp on Germany and the Netherlands, and which, like all such movements, looked unfavourably upon art in association with worship.

William of Ockham (*c.* 1300–50), the last great philosopher of the Middle Ages, provided a sharp weapon for critical thought and confirmed the sceptical trends of the time by his theory of knowledge. He denied that anything could be known except by experience. Religious belief therefore depended purely on an act of faith. His view, also, that God's decrees could be changed by His own will ran counter to the tradition which assumed a hierarchy of intermediary superhuman intelligences. He held that the whole physical world was a proper object of scientific investigation, and his ideas quickly found wide acceptance.

The scientific spirit was free to operate, although it had not yet acquired its systematic techniques and its guiding principles of thought. Even so, developments before the mid-15th century were momentous enough to bring the old world to an end and set the modern world on its course. By 1336 the Genoese had a settlement in China, and a hundred years later the Portuguese had sailed round Africa and opened the sea-route to India, an opportune achievement since the Turks in 1453 closed the ancient land-route to the East by finally taking Constantinople. The implications of world discovery were not by any means realized in this age, but the invention of the printing-press about 1450 bore more immediate fruit at a time when men were avid for knowledge. So too did the appearance of gunpowder and artillery. The French had to wait until the mid-15th century before they possessed a culverin which could out-shoot the English bowmen and bring to an end the squalid miseries of an age in which bands of mercenaries wasted her manhood and her countryside. Through Joan of Arc they found something more: the recovery of their morale. The English hold on France was broken before the advent of the gunners. It was not to be the last time that the spirit of man would prove more powerful than the mechanical products of his ingenuity.

To summarize: The changes in thought and behaviour which took place in these years throughout Europe sprang from two main causes. One was the loosening of the stranglehold which the Church had imposed in the name of Christianity; the other was the waning of feudal organization as society developed new activities and needs. The horizon of thought had widened immeasurably through the steady assertion of the claims of reason, and through increasing awareness of the finer civilization which had existed in antiquity. Commercial and professional success bred self-confidence in the individual and an urge to give expression to the many different promptings of his own mind. The abstractions of an all-embracing system faded in the light of living experience, thought, and imagination. Its lifeless symbols lingered on in quarters where feudal power had taken strongest hold, but the awakening human vision was apparent in the smaller communities, quickened in mind by their own achievements. Literature and painting are the arts which can most readily communicate the observation of human thought and experience, and it was in these that the new spirit found its first outlet. Following inevitably from freedom of self-expression, marked differences of taste and temperament emerged or were confirmed, and made their individual contributions to the general mind. This became apparent even in music, although that art was still mainly serving the needs of practical life in worship, dancing, entertainment, and conventional lyrics. The English note of seriousness and self-importance appears in the Agincourt Song, and their love of sonorous choral sound in cultivating singing in four or even five parts; the French showed

their addiction to logical subtleties in their isorhythmic structures, and the Italians their instinct for passionate melody. This
period's music, however, is more notable for flashes of inspiration
than for sustained corporate achievement.

In general, the South begins to blossom in sensuous expression,
and the North to reveal its critical and intellectual powers.
Europe is on the threshold of the Renaissance and the Reformation, and, through scientific and geographical discoveries, at the
beginnings of a phase of world expansion.

6

The Renaissance in Italy

I. The Visual Arts

"How many cities we saw as boys built all of wood which now are turned to marble!" In these words of Leon Battista Alberti (1404–72) we not only catch a glimpse of the physical transformation which the Renaissance was bringing to Florence and other Italian cities, but we sense something of the exalted enthusiasm which inspired the artists of the age. "The eyes especially by their nature are eager for beauty," he writes, and he and his contemporaries leave us in no doubt that a new world is opening before them, and that the departing age had been a dark interlude between the glories of antiquity and those which they themselves are intent to achieve. Alberti was typical of many men of the Renaissance; he was a writer, a theorist on the arts, and no mean practitioner himself. He embodied the spirit which for two centuries was to set Italy aglow, the conviction that truth should be sought in those realms of thought and activity which man could conquer by his own efforts, and that the way to those high realms lay through art and beauty. This vision of the artist was shared by teacher and idealist too; it was a new form of belief, not merely an aesthetic fashion. Where Christian faith had pointed to an ideal world of the spirit, the artist now showed these aspirations translated into human terms. He was no longer concerned with virtues and vices as abstractions, but with the portrayal of men and women who revealed in their reactions to life the infinitely varied interplay between high and low which actually exists in human experience. Leonardo da Vinci's well-known painting, *The Last Supper*, illustrates this humanized interpretation. Instead of the stiff traditional row of figures invested with the dignity of apostles, we see twelve living men at the dramatic moment when Christ has said "one of you shall betray me". The artist has re-lived the scene in his imagination so that he not only presents its external appearance, vivid as that is in detail and differentiated portraiture, but he penetrates to the inner character of every disciple. In showing each individual's reaction, he reveals an aspect of truth which we take for granted in the modern world: that the human mind is a complex of many variables, which cannot be permanently satisfied with the over-simplifications of medieval symbolism. This enlargement of view we owe to the Renaissance, and its painters were the first to follow the lead of Petrarch in illuminating the many facets of the human mind.

It is well to note the part played by the intellect in this great upsurge of art. The romantic notion that a work of art is created by a kind of spontaneous combustion, a welling up of emotion, or a passive reception of "inspiration", is a superficial view far too widely held. The urge to create, and the germ of the finished creation, come from the unconscious, but that is only the beginning of the artist's work. Everything else depends on his power and range of mind, and on his command of technique. No epoch shows more clearly than the Renaissance how the creative artist makes an instantaneous communication which transcends thought and emotion alike; it fuses the two, and produces its own dimension of human experience. Leonardo himself, as recorded by an eye-witness, would stand before his work thinking for a whole day without painting a stroke. The parallel case of Mozart comes to mind; he would silently bring a composition to maturity before committing its notes to paper. No "fine careless rapture" here; but in the final execution there is no doubt of the balance of mind and emotion which always distinguishes the greatest art of the world.

It is easy for us to see after the event that the painting, sculpture, and architecture of the Quattrocento, as the Italians call the 15th century, opened an era and gave a fresh orientation to the European mind. But for the artists themselves the task was a direct one: to gain mastery of their medium. The pioneers in painting were not educated men. They learnt their craft as apprentices in the workshops of master-painters, perfecting their technique in routine processes and inconspicuous parts of the master's work, until they were skilful enough to win their own commissions. In this respect they lived in a fortunate age of eager demand for civic, personal, and ecclesiastical splendour, and those who had genius—and how many there were in this century and in the succeeding Cinquecento—achieved a proud independence which enabled them to accept or reject commissions in the highest places. Genius is unpredictable, but there was a predisposition to artistic talent in the regions about Tuscany, an inherent taste which had perhaps persisted from the ancient days of the Etruscan civilization. However that may be, there were some practical problems for the men of the Quattrocento to solve, problems which arose from the new urge to paint what the eye sees, not what the mind knows to be there. For both sculptor and painter the human figure was the most absorbing subject, and the artists of the 15th century were engaged in learning the secrets of its natural portrayal. Study of anatomy supplemented direct observation, and the lessons of Gothic sculpture were not overlooked in seeking to create the illusion of depth on a flat surface. In painting, Giotto had made the decisive step in this direction at the beginning of the Trecento, from the spiritual world of the Byzantine mosaics, where "reality" lay behind the flat figures, to that of the dawning Renaissance where reality was to be sought in the figures themselves. In sculpture, Gothic art retained its vigour throughout the 14th and 15th centuries, and the Renaissance pioneers built on this foundation as well as on the study of the remains of antiquity. Ghiberti's famous bronze reliefs for the Baptistery gates at Florence (1402) continue this tradition. They form part of an architectural whole, but they achieve something new with their vivid pictorial character. The busy scenes with their backgrounds of trees and tents, their figures full of movement and gesture, seem likely to strain the medium to its extreme, but unfailing Florentine taste ensured the convincing unity of the panels with their environment.

Architectural reliefs and sculptured figures formed a large part of the work of Donatello (1386–1466), the predominant sculptor of the Quattrocento. With him, the Classical heritage is evident in the poise and purity of his art, and the Renaissance spirit in the balance between artistic form and the expression of human character. Within his classical limits, his range of feeling is wide, from the youthful fearlessness of his *St. George*, the tender and spiritual expression of the *Annunciation* in S. Croce at Florence (Plate 11), to the intensity of suffering shown in the features and the tensed muscles of his *Crucifix* in the same church. He enlarged the European horizon in still another way: his *David*, in the Bargello at Florence, is the first Renaissance sculpture in the round, the earliest of a long succession of works independent of architecture. This development came to its climax with Michelangelo (1475–1564), whose creations in marble sprang from, and communicate, a feeling of titanic energy. They embody the pride of the Renaissance in human vigour and vitality, its ideal of faithful representation of appearance and movement, and its interpretation of the mind and emotions of man through their visible bodily expression. Michelangelo brought to sculpture an intensity of feeling and a power of movement which, in the work of his successors, was to pass beyond the bounds of classical restraint; but with him, imagination still glowed within a convention which never failed to be purely artistic. In his *Pietà* in Florence Cathedral, the four figures are deeply moving in resigned and sorrowful expression yet superbly satisfying from any angle as a sculptural group. Again, his monumental sculpture in the Medici Chapel lives vividly in its human forms. It expresses the Renaissance cult of "fama" and grandiose aspirations to immortality through art, but the recumbent figures on the tombs are not merely individual monuments placed in an existing building, they are conceived with the memorial chapel itself as an artistic whole, harmonious in the proportions of its windows, panels and pilasters, its dome, arches, and every subsidiary detail.

This absorption in exploring the possibilities of natural expression and artistic form is close to the Greek conception, and certainly owed its existence to the Renaissance reverence for that ancient ideal and to the close study of surviving models. There is, however, a far greater range of expression in Italian sculpture, which reflects the deepened emotional experience which came to Europe through Christianity, with its contribution of devotion, tenderness, and suffering. Greek art was seeking idealized expression; the Renaissance did not fail to preserve much of that ancient ideal of nobility, but it had a richer emotional and spiritual tradition, and aimed at a more varied interpretation of human life.

Although sculpture is well able to convey feeling, it is primarily an art of form and shape. It was in painting that the European mind achieved its most intimate revelations in visual form. Continuing the tradition of religious narrative art (and adding scenes of pagan mythology as Classical learning spread among educated people), painters during the 15th century mastered the faithful representation of human anatomy. They had long since learnt to convey a sense of impersonal spirituality. Their aim now was to portray humanity in its active as well as passive experience. They began to place figures in lifelike relation to one another and their background. Knowledge of perspective was a necessary means to this end, and architectural backgrounds in countless pictures

show the interest it aroused, even to artificial excess, as in the
façade of the old Scuola S. Marco (now the Ospidale Civile), in
Venice, where apparently receding views are represented on flat
panels of stone. But the ultimate triumph of the Renaissance
painters was to achieve artistic form as well as lifelike representation. Pollaiuolo is clearly conscious of this aim in his *Martyrdom
of St. Sebastan* (National Gallery, London), where the six archers
are grouped with rather obvious symmetry around the martyr.
The solution of this problem in a natural way, before 1500,
crowned the achievements of the Quattrocento in the art of
picture-making, and it is at this point that the great masters of
the High Renaissance inherited the tradition. It is not by chance
that certain paintings have become household names through
widespread reproduction and reference: Leonardo's *Last Supper*
and *Mona Lisa*, Michelangelo's painting of the *Sistine Chapel
Ceiling*, Raphael's *Sistine Madonna*. They are part of our general
mind because they use the magic of art to illumine aspects of life,
of personality, of spiritual experience, which can be explored in
no other way. Neither words nor music can convey the powerful
sense of creation which Michelangelo achieves in his Sistine
Chapel painting, when the finger of God, without touching Adam,
awakens him to life. No other art can suggest the mystery of
personality as it appears in *Mona Lisa*, or lead the mind by lines
of composition, as in Raphael's *Galatea*, to the central feature of
a design.

There is little wonder that succeeding painters became intoxicated with the power of art. The opulent riches of Bellini,
Titian, Veronese, Correggio, Tintoretto, gave a sunset glow to
the Renaissance. Classical restraint was followed by dramatic
display, composition by line and subtle use of light and shade
was amplified and even replaced by sensuous delight in colour.
But as long as the true Renaissance character persisted, these
tendencies did not overstep the bounds of a convention which
demanded truth to nature, and at the same time, artistic selection
and concentration on the essential. Purity of form and taste
prevailed.

The ideal of pure form gave unique character to the architecture of the Renaissance. Beauty of design was the predominant
idea, not merely structural necessity, although in some cases
modifications of existing buildings had to be undertaken. Even
in these cases, the new taste, and the ancient sources of its
inspiration, are unmistakeable. For instance, one of the early

tasks of Alberti was to design an exterior marble facing for the existing Gothic church of S. Francesco at Rimini, to serve the ambitions of the Malatesta family. His debt to Roman architecture is obvious in the arch of the west door, which so strongly resembles the Arch of Tiberius, still surviving in that city. Another modification which the new taste imposed on an existing Gothic structure is evident at S. Maria Novella, Florence, where Alberti's marble façade incorporates rounded arches, a Classically inspired pediment, and an invention of his own in the curved volutes which mask the junction of the upper structure of the nave with the side-aisles (Plate 12). This innovation was to have a great subsequent development in Baroque architecture. But the most glorious of all blendings of Gothic and Renaissance structure is Brunelleschi's dome for the Cathedral of Florence, which employs Gothic principles of vaulting while springing from a new artistic vision. Like many of the architects of the Renaissance, Brunelleschi was a goldsmith and a sculptor, and brought a pictorial sense to his architectural creations. He, like Alberti, had made meticulous study and measurements of Roman remains, but he was no copyist. His work reveals the fertilizing influence of his studies of antiquity, and the absorption of fundamental principles of harmony and proportion. The exquisite chapel which he designed for the Pazzi family, and the Cloisters of S. Croce in Florence, show the new Renaissance character in its freshness and purity. Basic features of ancient arch and column, semicircular vault and horizontal entablatures underlie this new art, but there is a gracefulness and delicacy, above all a feeling of serene repose in the pure creations of the early Renaissance which place them on the highest planes of all art. This peaceful beauty is communicated by buildings small and large: intimate in S. Maria Formosa at Venice, or in Bramante's Tempietto at Rome, or grandly imposing as in S. Lorenzo at Florence, and in the late Renaissance Library by Sansovino, at Venice (Plate 13).

Simple, strong, and practical, yet able to incorporate many variations of detail, this architectural style remained basic throughout the High Renaissance; it provided the foundations of the Baroque elaborations which were to follow, and it remained, until the 20th century, as the model for imitation both inspired and otherwise, for all purposes of public life. Palaces and public buildings were their arcaded façades or courtyards, churches with their domes raised on drums decorated externally

by columns and windows, internally with coffered ceilings or
fresco paintings, walls divided by pillars and pilasters in symmetrical proportions and harmoniously spaced windows headed
alternately with shallow curves and pediments—all have become
part of the European environment, and have spread abroad as
our civilization has expanded overseas. To name their separate
features is to lose the essential quality of this art, which lies in
its perfect harmony, its immediate communication of artistic
experience, which nevertheless can be renewed unceasingly. Like
the sister arts of painting and sculpture, Renaissance architecture
reached a point of perfection which is recognized as "classic",
and then, passing through its phase of fullest flowering it ripened
into luxuriance and mannerism, or became stereotyped in
academic formulas. Before its zenith was passed it expressed the
mind of an age intoxicated with the joy of human power and
achievement, lavish in patronage, but above all rich in individual genius nourished by long artistic tradition. To think of
the Cathedral dome at Florence, St. Peter's dome at Rome, and
the Library of S. Marco at Venice (Plate 13) is to recall not only
Brunelleschi, Michelangelo, Sansovino, who created them, but
Florence's unfailing tradition of taste, the glowing warmth of
Venice, and the majesty and splendour of Rome. This unparalleled art did not come into existence just because there
happened to be an unusually large number of men of genius, as
well as workers in every subsidiary craft; the artists themselves
were created by the demand of the age. There can be no better
summary of this phase of the European mind than that given by
J. A. Symonds at the beginning of the third volume of his
Renaissance in Italy: "It has been granted only to two nations,
the Greeks and the Italians, and to the latter only at the time of
the Renaissance, to invest every phase and variety of intellectual
energy with the form of art. Nothing notable was produced in
Italy between the 13th and the 17th centuries that did not bear the
stamp and character of fine art. Not only was each department
of the fine arts practised with singular success; not only was the
national genius to a very large extent absorbed in painting, sculpture, and architecture; but the aesthetic impulse was more subtly
and widely diffused than this alone would imply. It possessed the
Italians in the very centre of their intellectual vitality, imposing
its conditions on all the manifestations of their thought and feeling, so that even their shortcomings may be ascribed in a great
measure to their inability to quit the aesthetic point of view."

7

The Renaissance in Italy

II. Thought and Literature

ITALY, in the Renaissance, looked to antiquity as the pattern of every kind of excellence. She liked to think of it as a glorious phase of her own history, and already spoke of the "Middle Age" as a dark interlude of Gothic barbarism which was past. Petrarch and his 14th-century successors, with their zeal for a way of life which would combine the noblest moral ideals of antiquity with the tenets of Christianity, had brought into being a Humanist movement whose emphasis was on the formation of character. Seeking all possible guidance to this end, the individualists of the early Renaissance could find no help in medieval scholasticism, which had ignored all that Greece and Rome could teach man about art and self-reliant conduct, and so they sought eagerly for Classical manuscripts as their source of information and inspiration. The quest continued into the 16th century. According to R. R. Bolgar, "most of the Latin and a substantial portion of the best Greek authors were in circulation by 1516. Thanks to the efforts of the Aldine Press, learning was no longer tied to the apron-strings of the copyist."

Possession of the Classical heritage was valueless in itself; the key to its use lay in educational method. Once again the mind of Europe was to submit to a new discipline and to make fresh contact with the mind of Greece, this time through the medium of Byzantium. The immediate link was the teaching of Manuel Chrysoloras, who visited Florence first on a diplomatic mission, but was induced, by humanist enthusiasm to return as a municipally paid lecturer in 1396. He had charm and scholarship, but above all he had a method of teaching. He kept alive the attitude of Gemistos Plethon, who had departed significantly from the long Byzantine tradition of studying the ancients only as models of style; his aim was to bring his own ideas into communion with those of antiquity. In this he was a pioneer of the Renaissance. Chrysoloras, who taught or corresponded with many leading scholars of the age, made a great impact on their minds. The essential feature of his method was attention to accurate use of language. Material collected in the course of reading was to be written down in a note-book; the student would then proceed from the easier authors to the more difficult orators and historians and use them as models for his own composition. This typically Byzantine method of imitation may seem to have limitations, but it was something new in the West, and, as it developed in the work of a succession of Humanists (Bruni, Guarino, Valla), it made the Latin legacy available to the mid-15th century public in convenient form, and it facilitated quick and correct composition. By the early 16th century Greek literature too was being assimilated, and the work of Erasmus spread the legacy, and the method of study, throughout Europe.

The value of this discipline was not merely literary. Although the Renaissance scholars were primarily seeking power of expression, and looking to heroes in antiquity to support their own ideology, they were absorbing at the same time the standards and modes of thought of a maturer civilization than their own, one which could offer abundant examples of self-sufficient human conduct. These ideals did not remain merely as scholarly aspirations, they passed into practical education. Vittorino da Feltre (1378–1446) has been called the first modern schoolmaster. He was no revolutionary. For him, Classical culture was not inconsistent with loyalty to the Church, but was a means of implanting ideas, developing taste, and of acquiring knowledge to enrich the Christian life. This was also the emphasis in the schools which carried his example into other countries, and combined as it was with care for physical development it differs little from the conception still familiar in British public schools. But if the new culture did not supplant Christian teaching, the Church no longer held a monopoly in education, and in the High Renaissance at the opening of the 16th century the new spirit of independence of authority could express itself in many Italian courts in a scarcely disguised paganism. The blatant worldliness and disregard of true morality, accompanied by a cynical observance of the outward forms of religion, were the fruits of an unbridled ʹassertion of individualism. The political theories of Macchiavelli (1469–1527), realist and opportunist, the egoism and violence revealed in Benvenuto Cellini's autobiography, and the atrocities of the Borgias are well-known examples of the seamy side of the age. Yet, at the other extreme from these abuses, and in fact provoked by their very existence, the spirit of critical independence was to find a completely different expression in the German Reformation. This movement, although so different in its aim and emphasis, was nevertheless an outcome of the Renaissance spirit and of the new techniques of education.

When untrammelled expression of individuality is the ruling motive, all kinds of human passion, from highest to lowest, will find their release. They had never been fully harnessed or suppressed, even while the Christian ideal commanded universal acceptance. They found unprecedented scope while the civic and ecclesiastical despots of Renaissance Italy had opportunity to exploit their own wealth and position, and when the mind of the age was set upon human self-glorification. The atmosphere of freedom bred excesses, but these passed away with their epoch, while the positive creations of the period still live in our cultural heritage. The greatest benefaction of this liberation of mind was in the glories of the visual arts, which still remain unique as they were then conceived and executed. But these were not its only fruits. Others, in the realm of ideas, are scarcely less real, even if the forms in which they were then held have been abandoned. They provided, as it were, a pivot on which the European mind turned from the old to the modern world. Thus, for example, the Renaissance produced no original philosophy but it broke the grip of scholasticism, and by reviving the study of Plato it "demanded at least so much independent thought as was required for choosing between him and Aristotle". (Bertrand Russell, *History of Western Philosophy*.) The realization that differing opinions can be held on the same subject promoted mental activity where passive acceptance had prevailed. Again, in science, no theory held in the Renaissance is fully tenable to-day. Copernicus (1473–1543) it is true, believed that the sun, not the earth, was the centre of the universe, a view which had awkward implications for traditional Christian theology, but in many respects his hypotheses were quite invalid. Yet his attitude approaches the modern one, that the test of scientific truth is patient collection of facts, and that views which have ruled unchallenged might well be proved to be false. In medicine, the collection of facts through dissection and through observation of patients laid the foundations of modern method, but theory did not get much further than leaning upon Hippocrates and Galen —antiquity was still sacrosanct. In the printing-press, Europe found the first of its modern means of mental communication;

through geographical discovery it became aware, in 1492, of the American continent in the west; while in the east, since the late 14th century, Slavs, Finns, Poles, and Lithuanians had been consolidating against Oriental enemies on the basis of a common Christian belief. These facts are significant, and obvious, to our modern mind; they scarcely affected that of the Renaissance.

The humanist movement in Italy came to a focus when Cosimo de' Medici, head of the great banking family which effectually ruled Florence, appointed Marsilio Ficino in 1459 to translate Plato into Latin. The community of students who gathered about him to share in a common life of contemplation became known as the Academy, and they applied their minds to all aspects of knowledge and of art. This universal kind of scholarship remained normal until the end of the 18th century, when a vastly widened range of knowledge made professional specialization inevitable. They therefore studied and expounded both the pagan Greeks, and the Christian Dante—a sign of the indeterminate position of the age, between different worlds of thought—and they duly cultivated such practical subjects as natural science, medicine, and astrology. We do not look to the Renaissance, however, for its thought expressed in philosophy but in art, and, in the case of the Florentine Academy, for its stimulating influence on all contemporary activity. Humanists visited it from Oxford, Paris, and Cologne, and through them and a gifted generation of Italian pupils, its ideals gave motive power to many important movements of the 16th century. Johann Reuchlin for instance, who had stayed in Florence, contributed to the thought of his friend Erasmus, and to Luther's movement, which founded its Bible study on the new reading methods of the Humanists.

More immediately, the aspirations of the Academy found expression in some notable works of civic humanism, and in Italy's fullest flowering of literary art. Ficino and Pico della Mirandola presented the purest ideal, seeking a way of life which would reconcile philosophy and religion. It is significant that the members of the Academy even supported Savonarola, in spite of his bigoted hatred of art and beauty, in his efforts to cleanse the civic life of Florence. Castiglione embodied the essential spirit of the Renaissance when he set forth in his *Cortegiano*, 1528, the qualities desirable in the ideal courtier: learning and good manners, chivalry and human dignity, and the exercise of his highest virtue as patron, philosopher, and poet.

Here is the pattern of social behaviour for Tudor England, exemplified by Elizabeth herself and by Sir Philip Sidney in his life and in his death. More realist and ruthless in application, yet expressing an objective political philosophy, Macchiavelli's *Il Principe* and Guicciardini's *History of Contemporary Italy* were early contributions to the science of man, turning away equally from medieval theology and the lofty idealism of academic minds. At the farthest remove from any ideal, Pietro Aretino (1492–1556) enjoyed great contemporary popularity, and subsequent execration, for his vivacious and scurrilous writings in many genres about the low life of the times, exercising a function similar to that of much unsavoury modern journalism. Such writing does not form part of the permanent European heritage, but no account of the mental climate of any age is balanced if it ignores the forms in which unregulated human behaviour finds expression. It was present in Classical literature, in the impromptus of goliard, minstrel, and trouvère, in the popular ribaldries which spiced the medieval mystery cycles, and now it reappears in this racy non-academic writing of the Renaissance, as it will in Rabelais, and in the drama of Spain and of Elizabethan England.

But this was not the central note of Italian Renaissance literature. Life, whether in its ideal or sordid aspects, yielded place to consciously artistic expression, for the most part with an excess of artificiality. The visual arts, not poetry, were the medium through which the Italian mind communicated its deepest intuitions about human experience. In literature, the tendency was to present separate aspects of life—the complete courtier, the single-minded politician, the figures of romance glittering as they do in Ariosto but always with superhuman beauty and prowess. The artistry is consummate, but it produces a world of illusion and a sentiment lacking in the sympathetic warmth which comes from the mingled strains of life. This is so especially in the copious Latin literature produced by the Humanist enthusiasm for antiquity. Rigid conventions ruled in poetry, and although great and influential prose works appeared both in Italy and the northern countries, the Renaissance could not catch the fervour of the great Latin hymn-writers of the Middle Ages. In the Italian language, greater heights were reached in poetry, with exquisite polish in Poliziano, sensuous and passionate expression in Lorenzo de' Medici and Michelangelo, but with a hardening into artificiality and convention in numerous Canzone and Madrigals, and above all in the lyric "Petrarchism" of Bembo. This kind of formalization seems to be inevitable in any period after its particular outlook has once found its zenith of spontaneous expression. But art never stands still, and even if Italian poetry depended too easily on external polish and elegant form, that was no loss to the general mind of Europe, since those were the very qualities which were of value to posterity, both as models of style and also as a discipline and inspiration in mastering highly wrought forms. It was not for nothing that Europe, until 1800, looked back to this period as a golden age of literature.

Lyric poetry was only one part of the legacy. Italy now entered a field which she, alone among the European nations, had left uncultivated in the Middle Ages, that of the epic. She did so with her characteristic individualism and sophistication. In fact Pulci (1432–84), the first in the field with his *Morgante*, treated the Charlemagne stories with levity and irreverent burlesque. After him, Boiardo (1441–94), in the service of the Este court at Ferrara, where lip-service was paid to chivalry, gave serious treatment in his *Orlando innamorato* to the popular stories which Pulci had treated with levity. Midway between these attitudes, Ariosto (1474–1533), a far greater figure, ranged from romance to irony in his *Orlando furioso* (1516), which re-tells the story of Roland, or rather, weaves an intricate web of many stories taken from romantic legends well known to his contemporary readers. This first great landmark of 16th-century poetry captivated the mind of Europe for centuries, giving delight by the ease of its narrative, by the charm of its verse and its gentle mockery, but more significantly by an attitude which modern man recognizes as his own. Where Boiardo had constant recourse to magic and the fabulous, where the medieval *chansons de gestes* assumed the inevitable victory of Christian over infidel as a just ordinance of providence, Ariosto gave weight to human motives and observed their influence on events. When a Saracen army, excited by victory, is at the gates of Paris, far from exploiting its strong position, it halts and disintegrates, not through any external intervention but simply through its own unresolvable discords and conflicts of opinion. There is a touch of allegory in attributing this victory to "Discord", but the abstraction is clearly a symbol of motives which reside in man himself. The classicists of the Cinquecento found Ariosto's *Orlando furioso*, with its humour and its humanity, deficient in those "elevating" qualities

11. Donatello: Annunciation. Mid 15th century. S. Croce, Florence.

12. S. Maria Novella, Florence. Facade by L. B. Alberti, 1456–1470.

13. The Library of St. Mark's Venice. Sansovino, 1536.

and gravity of thought which should belong to a truly Virgilian epic. Pope Leo X, in commissioning a cleric called Vida to write a *Christiad*, appears to have entertained similar doubts about the New Testament story itself. This attitude is a sign of hardening conventions which were to attain complete rigidity in the subsequent classicism of France. Vida and his contemporaries evolved a theory of the epic which left its mark on the work of Tasso (1544–95), the last great poet of the Italian Renaissance. His first work, *Rinaldo* (1562), conforms to the Classical demand for unity in its single hero and plot, but in his greatest work, *Gerusalemme liberata*, the poet is impelled to transcend the limitations of any Classical formula by his overriding passion. The epic is a romantic treatment of the First Crusade, with all the set scenes of the ancient models, and all the apparatus of battles, marvels, and noble sentiments. Glory and love are its themes; but there is no doubt which is the more urgent in Tasso's mind. He wrote himself: All beautiful things are fitting for the heroic poem, "but the most beautiful is love". He takes obvious delight in the sensuous element, whether it be the charms of a garden or the softer side of love, and in this subjective leaning he shows his affinity with the modern rather than the ancient or medieval mind.

In feeling the attraction of natural beauty so strongly while concerned with the sterner themes of war and piety, Tasso shared with his compatriots a sentiment which developed very understandably in environments where intrigue and violence prevailed — a nostalgia for rural peace. Whether genuine or in some degree superficial, this longing found expression in pastoral idylls and plays which fertilized the art of Europe not only in poetry but in the painting of such as Poussin and Watteau, and most decisively for the future of music in the 17th-century transition to opera. The pastoral tradition was an ancient one in literature, and the idylls and dialogues of Theocritus and Virgil were very much alive in the thoughts of Renaissance poets. Poliziano brought something of this atmosphere into the *sacra rappresentazione*, or Italian mystery play, in his *Orfeo* (1480), but the work which released a flow of activity in this genre was Sannazaro's *Arcadia* (1489), with its gentle melancholy and aristocratic feigning of pleasure in simple rural delights. Tasso's pastoral drama *Aminta* (printed in 1581) rose far above the mere conventions of pastoralism into a world of intense feeling, though its successor, the *Pastor fido* of Guarini, provided the formula which served for general imitation. It was in the pastoral or lyrical play that Italy made her individual contribution to the European theatre. In the purer drama she depended too closely on the classical models of Plautus and Terence in comedy, and Seneca in tragedy; her true genius was to find its outlet when the full range of human emotion became the subject of musical drama in the 17th century and replaced the nymphs and shepherds of Arcadia.

8

The Renaissance outside Italy
Reformation and Counter-Reformation

I

THE Renaissance took mainly an artistic form in Italy. Its
particular character in that country owed much to continuity of
tradition, to the pride of kinship with ancient Rome, and to
unique qualities of taste and temperament. It also owed not a
little to the fact that neither the feudal system nor Gothic art
and architecture had taken firm root in the peninsula. Conditions
were different elsewhere in Europe. Although there was the same
sense of awakening and of discovering new mental and moral
attitudes; although the stimulating example of Italy's own
achievement was there for all to see, the spirit of renewal acted
on different temperaments and in varied environments to produce
quite distinctive results and a diversity of character which gave
strength and splendour to the European heritage. As always, the
intellectual emphasis was stronger in the North, and the sensuous
more evident in the South. In particular, the German and the
Spanish minds now made their first original contributions to
European experience, the first through Luther's Reformation
movement, the second as the principal agent of reaction against
that movement. The Reformation and the Counter-Reformation,
in their purest aspects, gave expression to the moral ideals and
the newly awakened conscience of Europe. But they did not make
their impact in that simplest form; from the first, they were
associated with personal and political rivalries in a Europe where
constant manœuvre for a balance of powers had replaced the
medieval conception of universal authority. They were products
of the general European re-nascence, in the sense of re-birth; they
in their turn determined the local forms taken by the Renaissance
in culture and in the arts.

The historical facts of the German Reformation are well
known. Martin Luther's dramatic challenge of old assumptions

and current abuses launched a movement which by 1520 had become defined as a new religion. Thenceforward, Protestantism existed with Catholicism as a rival form of Christianity. This division of the Christian mind of Europe did not arise solely from religious conviction, sincere as that was with many thinking people. It reflected also the social and political conditions of the time. Many secular princes, critical of clerical exactions and privileges, were ready to support a cause which coincided with their own worldly interests. On the other side, the young Habsburg Charles V, Holy Roman Emperor and King of Spain, enjoyed an unprecedented power in Catholic lands. He, and later his son Philip II, were the champions of the older faith throughout the 16th century, using the soldiery of Spain and the newly instituted powers of the Jesuit Order and the Inquisition to confirm both their own dominion and that of Rome. Their régime, to be followed in the 17th and 18th centuries by the supremacy of the rival Bourbon family in France, sharpened still further the difference between northern and southern Europe, the former largely Protestant, the latter almost solidly Catholic. Even within Germany itself, the old political divisions prevented anything like total adoption of a national Protestant religion, although Luther enjoyed the support of the printing-press and of a great part of the German people. Until 1648, when the Treaty of Westphalia secured a compromise of exhaustion, dynastic and religious feuds brought years of confusion, misery, and devastation, which delayed the development of Germany for still another two hundred years.

Sectarian divisions also, from the earliest days of the new religion, produced divergences of thought and practice which have remained characteristic of Europe. Inevitably so, since rejection of the Catholic dogma and assertion of individual judgment is of the very nature of the Protestant faith. Zwingli brought independence, both political and religious, to Switzerland, where Calvin was to give logical definition and austerest practice to the faith, and to make Geneva a centre of influence, especially for the Huguenots of France and the dour believers of Scotland. Bohemia and the Scandinavian countries began to develop their individuality, and the English found their own distinctive compromise between Church and State, and were to become nearly as prolific as the Dutch in finding subtle differences which loomed, for the believer, as large as heaven and hell.

The general tendency, among all the denominations of the reformed religion, was to intellectual rather than artistic effort. Theological exposition was dear to their hearts; ritual and aesthetic contributions were variously regarded. The severest pietists frowned upon it all. Yet among the noblest and most enthralling treasures of our English language are Cranmer's Prayer Book and the Authorized Version of the Bible. Luther's dynamic writings, and his Bible version, laid the foundations of the modern German language, and Calvin's translation of his own *Institutiae* ranks high even amid the eloquence of his native France. Above all, the German *chorale* was close to the hearts of the Lutheran worshippers. Ancient church melodies and contemporary compositions, native tunes both sacred and secular, some of great beauty, some dull and pedestrian, but all acquiring a ponderous grandeur and a depth of meaning and association which made them a symbol of the word of God, helped both to spread the faith and to contribute to its greatest consummation in the work of Johann Sebastian Bach.

The Reformation was the product of various trends which had developed over several generations, but it came to a focus through the decisive action of one man, Martin Luther, and in Germany it continued to bear the stamp of his personality. The forces of opposition to the Protestant movement also drew their strength from diverse political sources and from the established institutions of the Church, but they owed their first mobilization to the vision and initiative of one man, Ignatius Loyola. A soldier turned religious zealot and ascetic, he was ordained priest, and became the first head of the Jesuit Order, a militant body of dedicated men, prepared to carry out any task with efficiency, patience, and ruthlessness, and destined to exert a far-reaching influence in Europe through the power of education and of the confessional. The success of their movement in the vanguard of the Counter-Reformation is attested by the number of Jesuit churches which were built in the next two centuries, from Spain in the south-west to Poland and Russia in the east. The autocratic and secular direction of Catholic reaction was centred in the person of the Emperor, Charles V.

A new pattern of European life was emerging, one of princely absolutism associated with the ancient Catholic régime. It rested for more than a century to come on the infantry, the gold, the far-flung possessions of Spain, on the missionary and diplomatic efforts of the Jesuits, and on the cruel sanctions of the Inquisition.

This was the armoury of the Counter-Reformation. The Council of Trent, meeting at intervals between 1545 and 1563 restored some moral tone to ecclesiastical life and defined once more the doctrine of the Church. The Catholic mind and absolutist pattern of behaviour were now firmly determined. They were set rigidly against the restless forces of Protestantism, which in principle stood for the free expression of individual thought, but in practice tended to a narrow and bigoted outlook. The mind of Europe was to be darkened by the evil of intolerance until, in a calmer age of reason, the factions could at length agree to differ.

II

Against this background of religious fanaticism and schism, the vitalizing spirit of the Renaissance made its influence felt in all the countries of Europe. The German Reformation itself was in large part a product of this spirit, this newly developing capacity for criticism and constructive thought. It was nourished by Humanist studies, and in turn it gave inexhaustible energy to the pursuit of learning, and perpetuated a tradition of meticulous scholarship peculiar to Germany and Holland. German students who returned with Latinized names from the Italian Universities were not interested in beauty, but in moral and intellectual problems, in theological criticism, and the study of language. They returned to a country which lacked the Mediterranean instinct for harmonious form. Its strength lay rather in the crafts and minor arts, in printing and book-binding; in organ-building; in carving and sculpture in stone, wood, and metal which was still enriching their Gothic churches and civic buildings. German architecture was beginning to acquire Renaissance features, but rather as excrescences than as parts of harmonious ensembles. The Hofhaltung at Bamberg (Plate 14) show the mixture, with the typical stepped gables tapering to a summit, and details of Classical and Italian origin are jumbled together to produce an incongruous but imposing whole. The true harmony of Renaissance structure was to reach Germany far later, in the 18th century, with the magnificence of Rome and Versailles for its inspiration. The architecture of the Netherlands shows something of the same piecemeal adaptation of Renaissance features to their own characteristic gabled buildings of brick. The new Jesuit churches under the Spanish occupation of the 16th and

17th centuries were the first to bring a unified style from the south.

In painting, German artists of the early 16th century reflected the gravity and factual observation of their race, as well as pronounced traits of the medieval tradition. The old emphasis on suffering and martyrdom persisted with Grünewald and Cranach, though the latter shares with Altdorfer a new interest in landscape—a sign of interest in painting for its own enjoyment and not only for its religious message. Holbein's great altar-painting of the *Virgin with the family of Burgomeister Meyer* (1528), at Darmstadt, reveals the true Renaissance genius in its harmonious composition and fully human expression, as well as the northern love of detail and rugged features. But this master's career in Germany was ended by the new Reformation outlook. Through the recommendation of Erasmus he came to England, and as court painter to Henry VIII he established the art of portraiture, the only branch of painting which in this country survived the Reformation. Albrecht Dürer's work (1471–1528) was more deeply rooted in the Gothic tradition, although he, first among the Germans, came to share the southern fascination with the proportions of the human body. He showed his real affinity with the mind of his generation, seriously perturbed by the spiritual bankruptcy of the clergy, in his series of woodcuts illustrating the Book of Revelation and the terrors of doomsday.

The same preoccupation of an artist's mind with thought of impending retribution accounts for the fantastic visions of the terrors of hell conjured up by Hieronymus Bosch, a Dutch painter who died in 1516. This art, emphasizing the tortured and punitive aspects of medieval religion, seems utterly remote from the serenity of the Netherlands painting of the 15th century, pure and spiritual in its religious faith, or portraying with affectionate detail the scenes of domestic life. Even that endearing art was remote from the conception which ruled in Renaissance Italy. Michelangelo expressed the Classical view in his reported judgment on Flemish painting: "It aims at rendering minutely many things at the same time, of which a single one would have sufficed to call forth a man's whole application." The northern artists, realist, practical, and usually associated with busy trading communities, were less interested in purely artistic composition than in reflecting the life they saw around them. But from the mid-16th century they moved closer to the Renaissance ideal. Pieter Brueghel (1525–69) still gives us crowded scenes; his purpose is to illustrate human character, as revealed in peasant life throughout the seasons, but his method is no less an artistic one, as the arrangement of his figures shows. Our eye moves from one group or person to another, compelled by his subtle relationships. More still he brings a new meaning to landscape. It is no longer merely a background, but a scene in which people are really living their life. To move from this world into that of Peter Paul Rubens (1577–1640), is to step into the brilliant life of the late Renaissance. Yet, although Rubens' scenes and personages are far removed from peasant life, the trend which was seen in Brueghel is now fully established in a matured art of composition. Michelangelo himself introduced the opulent manner with his Sistine Chapel ceiling; his Italian successors, especially in Venice, richly exploited this vein, but none surpassed the easy mastery of the Flemish aristocrat who brought the tradition, fully developed, to Antwerp. Although late in time, delayed by the war against Spain, the consummation of the Renaissance in the Low Countries is the work of Rembrandt (1606–69). Undistracted by thoughts of Classical antiquity he is steadfast in his northern love of the homely scene. But no painter shows more power of artistic concentration, or deeper penetration of the human soul. No artifice appears, but by the supremest art light glows upon the features of his characters, so still, but so uncannily alive in surroundings which are felt rather than observed. Here, among the commerce and canals of Amsterdam, the same spirit which had been stirring the idealists of the Italian Renaissance was working—to seek through art the inner spirit of man.

III

Rubens and his pupil, Vandyck, shine out in exceptional and courtly splendour against the general drabness of the artistic scene in the Protestant countries. In fact they do not belong to the sober world of the Reformation but reflect the richer life of the Counter-Reformation during the Spanish occupation of the Netherlands. The influences of the Italian Renaissance had come to Spain at a time when the union of Castile and Aragon, and successful action against Moor and Jew, had promoted a sense of national and Christian unity. The Renaissance brought its full measure of artistic inspiration, but its spirit also chimed with that of the newly united people and contributed to the liberation of the whole national genius. This found its fullest expression in literature and drama, but the creative spirit affected individuals in all the other arts. In music, Morales and Victoria became masters of polyphony at Rome, and Cabezon contributed significantly to new developments in keyboard technique. Velazquez (1599–1660), court painter to Philip IV at Madrid, absorbed the lessons both of the pure Renaissance artists and those of their more dramatic successors, Titian, Rubens, and Caravaggio. But he made an individual contribution through suggestive effects of brushwork (in contrast with the meticulously detailed drawing of the northern painters) which gives a hint of the Impressionist technique of the 19th century. In her medieval architecture Spain had adopted the forms of French Gothic with fanciful ornamental elaborations of her own. In the new phase of church building which followed the expulsion of the Moors in 1492, Italian influences became all-pervasive, and as elsewhere in Europe, Renaissance details were incorporated with existing forms. In the first half of the 16th century this combination with earlier Moorish fancies produced a highly individual style known as Plateresque (like silversmiths' work). Building between 1550 and 1650 assumed a more austere and classical character, modelled on the purer forms of antiquity; the imposing mass of the Escurial belongs to this phase. After the mid-century, reaction against formalism led the Spanish architects to uninhibited enjoyment of a highly decorative and fantastic Baroque which belongs to Spain alone. It took the name of Churrigueresque, from its chief exponent.

It was through literature, however, especially in the form of fiction and drama, that all aspects of the Spanish mind were revealed. A particular quality of realism, both in observation and acceptance of life, stands out as central in their attitude. With this went a close relationship between art and life. Medieval epics and romances had retained their vitality in a kind of folk-tradition of verse and song. Cut down from their lengthy originals, they had become short epic-lyric poems known as *romanceros*, sung to an instrument and performed during choral dances and communal work. Spain's golden age of literature owed much of its strength to the blending of this popular stream with that of cultivated art, both in poetry and on the stage. Her language too preserved its colloquial directness even when enriched by the Latinity and the lyrical forms adopted from Italy. The stage is the natural outlet for such a broadly based human art. Fifty years before the full spate of literary activity began, a remarkable work appeared in 1499, called *La Celestina*, variously described as a fourteen-act play or as a novel in dialogue form. Its personages are of this world; its events arise inevitably from their respective natures, not from a prearranged plot. Such a realization of the implications of human character was new in literature; so was the stark realism which depicted two passionate lovers, the bawd Celestina who brought them together, and the scenes and minor characters which surround them. The work was widely translated and had its effect on European literature. The vast output of plays during the next century and a half indicates an absorbing interest in the theatre and a lively faculty for objective observation. It demanded also a technique of theatrical presentation, and Europe is indebted to Spain for several of the conventions of her dramatic art, as well as for an immensely widened range of subject and character. To most people outside Spain it may be that Lope de Vega, Tirso de Molina, Calderón, are little more than names; that no play of theirs comes to mind among the universal works of genius. The absence of tragedy also places a great gulf between their work and that of the Elizabethan or French dramatists. The Spanish theatre on the whole inclined to formalism. It depended largely on types like the "cloak and sword" play, the religious melodrama, the mythological spectacle; stereotyped motives like the "point of honour"; stock figures like the "gracioso" or peasant clown. But to mention the latter is to recall a lively succession of Figaros without whom European drama would be unthinkable. To name such formal innovations as the prologue, the interlude, the ballet accompanied by singing, is to recognize elements which have particular significance for future developments in opera, and through that medium for the whole art of music. Formalism indeed is indispensable when an artistic convention arises from constant public demand. The Italian opera, the Lutheran church cantata, the classical symphony and chamber music, were to provide examples of similar liaison between artist and audience.

The other medium through which the Spanish mind displayed its genius for shrewd and satirical observation was the *novela*. It owed much to the earlier imaginative fiction of Italy, and to the stream of social satire running, perennially fresh, through antiquity and the Middle Ages. The special invention of Spain was the picaresque novel, an imaginary autobiography used for ironic comment by the "picaroon", or social parasite. *Lazarillo de Tormes* (about 1554) was the first of a line which maintained its fertility both in Spain and abroad, for instance through Defoe (*Moll Flanders*), Fielding (*Jonathan Wild*), Le Sage (*Gil Blas*), and which is unlikely ever to become extinct. Beside these satires and other quasi-novels of manners, the romance of adventure and the pastoral romance gave scope to the Spanish imagination. Cervantes (1547–1616), the greatest genius of Spain, made use of them all, but his *Don Quixote* (1605 and 1615) fits into no fictional classification. Setting out to ridicule not merely the books of chivalry, which were already out of fashion, but rather the contemporary excesses of pride and scorn of all useful work, Cervantes created a character who has endeared himself to all by his nobility and generous idealism, one who came to believe in his own world of dreams, but was gently and inevitably led to realize that they were illusory. This work is a conception of a mind which neither accepts the affirmations of the Middle Ages nor shares the Renaissance confidence in man's self-sufficiency. It sounds a note more familiar to the modern mind; or is it not true that works of highest genius are of no age and of all ages?

Drama and the novela are concerned with the external scene. The more intimate art of lyric poetry was also quickened by the buoyant spirit of the nation during this creative era. Boscán, Garcilaso, Luis de Leon, Herrera; the Portuguese Camões too, whose *Os Lusiadas* was an epic of recent sea-faring history; all contributed to the splendour of the age. They took the forms newly learnt from Italy—the sonnet, terza rima, ottava rima—vitalized them with the directness of their native speech, and restored a warmth of poetry to forms which had hardened into Petrarchan conventions. Some splendid prose was also produced by fervent mystical writers revealing a tendency to practical morality rather than to the ecstasy of the late medieval Germans. But the range of humanist thought was narrowed and the free expression of mind inevitably stifled under the compulsions of the Inquisition, the Index, and the ubiquitous Jesuit Order. There was little stimulus to imaginative adventure amid the solemn ritual of a bigoted Court. And once more, in poetry itself, the decadence which seems inevitably to overtake all great epochs of art appeared in the mannerisms, metaphors and rhetoric which are associated especially with Góngora (1561–1627), the last poet of the age. As with his contemporary, Marino in Italy, his name became synonymous with a precious and enigmatical style.

IV

The great age of Spain came to its close in 1648 when the Treaty
of Westphalia signalled the failure of her bid to control the
politics of Europe. In her place, the newly emerging power of
France was to create the environment for the next phase of
European life, thought, and art. That culture was to radiate from
the court of a monarch who could claim that *"l'etat c'est moi,"*
but France experienced two hundred years of varying fortune
before she emerged from the devastations of the Hundred Years
War to that position of absolutism. Through her very pre-
eminence in medieval civilization her feudal barons and the
burghers of her towns were slow to shed their ancient ways of
life. Charles VIII's military incursion into Italy in 1494 first
opened the eyes of France to the wonders of the Renaissance
world, and social and political contacts during the following
century ensured the gradual assimilation of the new ways of life
and art. But medieval forms remained singularly assertive in
France. Italian artists and workmen were employed from the
early 16th century, to the chagrin of native craftsmen, but after
the stage of merely ornamental imitation was past, France began
to evolve an architecture, neither Gothic nor fully Renaissance,
which aptly expressed her character in that epoch. The châteaux
of the Loire—medieval fortresses in part and palaces, too, for increasingly luxurious living—reveal this transformation of a rude
barony into a civilized aristocracy. Gothic churches continued to
be built as late as the 17th century, with the traditional plan,
high roofs and vaults, but with Italian carvings filling every
available space. From the mid-century the absorption of Renaissance forms, and Roman orders, harmonious façades, pediments
and balustrades, proceeded rapidly, stimulated both by theory
(Serlio's Treatise published at Lyons) and by the practice of a
generation of architects returning from their studies in Rome.
The Palace of the Louvre in Paris, begun in 1546 and undergoing successive developments until 1878, is a record of this
process, and a reminder of the continuing vitality of the
Renaissance impulse. Signs of the individual French spirit
appeared in vivacious and copious ornament, always regulated
by taste and wit. Goujon and Cousin were pre-eminent in
sculpture which combined grace with Gallic verve. Painting was
virtually non-existent until the 17th century, but the minor arts
and the interior decorations on the one hand, and great formal

parks and courts on the other gave a foretaste of the luxury which was to follow, and prepared the scene for the courtly manners and theatrical display of the grand siècle.

Above all, in her fascinating literature of the 16th century France reveals the many facets of her mind. The strength of her medieval tradition is again apparent. As recently as 1461, Villon had written his *Testament*, and only at the end of the century were the old mystery plays giving place to farces and interludes. The memory of the rascally lawyer in *Maître Pierre Pathelin* (1464) was still fresh in the minds of the readers of Rabelais' *Pantagruel* in 1532. This strain of realism and satire is strong, and fortunately ineradicable in the national character. But confronted with the polish of Italian and Classical poetry, the French could not fail to be self-conscious about the uncouthness of their medievalism. They first attempted to improve their language by cultivating Latinisms and attempting a French equivalent of Classical measured scansion. But the real Renaissance spirit first appeared when Clément Marot, and then, more fully, Ronsard and the "Pléiade" reacted against the pedantry of a merely literal humanism. Ronsard (1524–85) and du Bellay achieved a grace and lucidity which were born of true poetic genius. After their first enthusiasm for Classical mythology and poetic forms they learnt to speak directly with human feeling. Their lyricism abounds in variety of form, rhyme, and metre; they established the Alexandrine, enriched the diction and rhythms of their language, and made it an expressive medium for either personal or generalized thought. Their own work remains fresh, but it also reveals, in its conscious elevation of style, the traits of a nation which was to become proud, and justly so, of its academic standards in literature. These were to be pushed to artificial extremes by Malherbe (1555–1628) and Boileau in the 17th century, but the French sense of style had already disclosed itself in every branch of literature in the mid-16th century: in Rabelais' phenomenal command of varied language, in Montaigne's apparently artless reflections, in the vigorous and polished satires of Regnier, and in the firm clear diction which was Malherbe's real gift to the Classical dramatists of the following age. Drama itself moved from the market-place to the literary stage, from the *sotties* of Gringoire and the fading Middle Ages, to tragedy and comedy which brought the art of antiquity to the service of the modern theatre. Translations from Italian preceded the first original works in the 'fifties, and the

Spanish comedies of intrigue mingled their influence with the stream. Before the end of the century Robert Garnier was writing tragedies with assurance, on the basis of the Classical unities, and the French stage was already rich in experience when Corneille began his work.

The Renaissance brought to France models of artistic form and thought which were especially congenial to her own genius. In her literature of the 16th century she displayed, over a wide range, those qualities of order and lucidity, pointed wit and elegant phrase, in which she is pre-eminent. But she also produced in François Rabelais (c. 1490–1553) one of those men of genius whose mind embraces all the experience of an age but passes far beyond it in range and penetration. In his five books of burlesque romance centred upon the giants Gargantua and Pantagruel, the scenes and figures are of the Middle Ages, the coarseness is that of the *fabliaux*, the satire is often directed at monasticism and degraded traditions of education. But the vast erudition is that of a Renaissance humanist. Rabelais calls upon the whole store of human knowledge, ancient, medieval, and contemporary. He revels in it unceasingly in quotation and amplification, and with imaginative force in the fantastic character of Panurge, an all-embracing but quite unmoral intellectualist. He shows his sympathy with Renaissance ideals in education, but it is precisely here that his mind is wider than the formulated thought of his day. He sees the vanity of man's pretensions; with his broad human sympathies he can ridicule them with indulgent humour. But he is sceptical of social idealism, and with Gallic irony he is only prepared to envisage a tolerable future for an educated minority whom he places in the solitude of a humanist retreat. A similar scepticism appears in Montaigne (1533–92), the earliest of all essayists. Like Rabelais he is one of the first Europeans to question both the assumptions of dogma and of Renaissance individualism. What do we know? All things are relative and man cannot judge. He ranges widely in comment and speculation, but he remains a highly civilized individual in the seclusion of his own study. In contrast, Rabelais, by the sweep of his imagination and the gusto of his humour, gives us the universal view of mankind and takes his place among the greatest figures of his age. "What Ariosto is for Italy, Cervantes for Spain, Erasmus for Holland, Luther for Germany, Shakespeare for England, that is Rabelais for France. The Renaissance cannot be comprehended in its true character without familiarity with these six representatives of its manifold and many-sided inspiration." (J. A. Symonds, in the *Encyclopædia Britannica*.)

v

The Renaissance came to England later than to the rest of Europe. It found its earliest expression in humanist scholarship (More's *Utopia*, in Latin, appeared in 1516) and in the educational work of a group of Cambridge scholars. Before it flowered in our greatest period of art, the national genius revealed itself in a typical compromise. The monarchy became both the symbolic and the *de facto* head of the Protestant Church of England and of a landed gentry made docile by the acquisition of former monastic property. This peaceful transition, and also the assertion of independence against threats of continental domination, contributed much to the extraordinary freedom of mind and lightness of spirit which marked the golden age of Elizabeth. At the same time, it strengthened the national tendency to insularity, and helped to consolidate a way of life based upon farming, industry, and trade, and seafaring activities which were later to carry that way of life to every corner of the world. It ensured the continuity of ancient institutions which still enrich our life; some also which were destined to influence the general mind of Europe. Our medieval parliament and common law, our universities, public schools and grammar schools, our ecclesiastical and parish organizations, our strong sense of the dignity of the individual; these, with their pageantry, the tranquil beauty of cathedral service and song, the late Gothic architecture of cathedral, church, and college, the timbered roofs so suggestive of the craftsmanship of a nation of sailors, the strangely individual Jacobean style—all belong to a specially English tradition. They are a heritage which we do not owe to the Italian Renaissance but rather to a quiet transformation of our own medieval institutions in the spirit of renewal which was stirring throughout Europe.

Although this continuity of character and institution runs as an unbroken strand through English history, the artistic glories of the Elizabethan age could not have been attained without the inspiration and example of the Italian poets and authors. By 1603 almost the whole range of Classical literature had been absorbed, more by way of translation from Italian and French than from the original sources. But as early as 1527, the poetry of Italy had fired the enthusiasm of Sir Thomas Wyatt who returned from that country with a desire to model our national verse on its metres and forms. He attained a regularity of rhythm and structure which had been in abeyance since Chaucer; he exploited new stanzas and rhyming schemes, and most important of all he introduced the Italian sonnet, through which our poets learnt the discipline of artistic concentration. His contemporary, the Earl of Surrey, besides exemplifying the Renaissance ideal of the gentleman and poet, was the first to use blank verse, the ten-syllable unrhymed line which became the medium for Elizabethan drama, infinitely flexible either for dialogue or for the highest flights of imagination. Flexibility indeed was the hallmark of this age, when so many tributaries were flowing into the stream of our thought and of our language. The English tongue had long since achieved a unique fusion of Germanic and Latin elements, in airiness and wit in Chaucer's literary springtime, a force and pithiness in common usage. With Tyndale's New Testament translation (1535), and Cranmer's Book of Common Prayer (1549), it acquired a noble music, rich in varied rhythms and modulated sounds which could not fail, by their regular recurrence to imprint themselves on the memory. With such an inheritance there was no danger of artificial imitation when the poets schooled themselves in the polished and intricate forms of the ancients and of the Italians. They steeped themselves in Classical history and mythology; they found endless resources of plot, convention, and character in the Italian romances and *novellieri*; they learned to manipulate the forms. But they did so as Englishmen, exhilarated with life and opportunity, proud of their nation, of their poetic calling, and of their language. They applied themselves, in Sir Philip Sidney's words "that we may bend to the right use both of matter and manner, whereto our language gyveth us great occasion". Far from accepting academic rulings, they took their booty as it came to hand, much as Raleigh, Drake, and Hawkins were doing on the high seas. Discussing our "mingled language" Sidney continues "for Grammar it might haue but it needs it not; being so easie of it selfe, and so voyd of those cumbersome differences of Cases, Genders, Moodes, and Tenses, which I think was a peece of the Tower of Babilons curse, that a man should be put to schoole to learne his mother-tongue". (*Apologie for Poetrie*, 1595.)

Merely to name the poets and playwrights of this prolific age would add a disproportionate catalogue to this brief European review. Even to indicate the main channels through which Elizabethan inspiration flowed; even to recall the salient qualities of the most outstanding figures, would do scant justice to the genius of the age. But in any survey of the European scene, Sidney and Spenser must take their place. The former, despite his capricious ornaments and subtleties, brought human passion into our poetry, and an ardour for artistic beauty. The latter, with the same qualities in good measure, gave to England the pageantry and descriptive beauty which she was denied through her lack of painters. His *Shepheard's Calendar* in 1579 gave the initial poetic impetus and confidence to his generation. The *Faerie Queene*, allegory, romance, descriptive poem, gathered a strangely assorted harvest from the mind and imagination of Europe in every phase of its history. The interest of the poem lies less in its thought and allegory than in the sustained beauty of its verse and the pictorial imaginings of its dream world. In the music of its diction, the all-embracing spectacles of its characters, scenes, and dances, it has kinship with the *masque,* and so presages that later stage of the literary Renaissance when poetry and drama were to call upon the emotional power of music to enhance their own effect. In his *Epithalamium*, Spenser created one of those perfect works which belong to all time; it is a poem unsurpassed in any literature. It was one of the glories of that volcanic age that it threw up isolated peaks of this kind, in the lyrics, sonnets, and drama of a succession of poets far into the 17th century. But it is the individual glory of Shakespeare that he moved so easily and so often in these rarer regions, and that he reached them in every literary form he used. The prodigal riches of poetry in the blank verse of his plays; the perfection of their lyrics and their emotional aptness in dramatic contexts; the great sequence of Sonnets expressing the passions both of the poet and of all humanity; these give him the pre-eminence which Milton accorded:

"Others abide our question, thou art free"

Apart from these highest flights, poetry in every genre abounded, and its spirit of exaltation pervaded prose as well as verse. In fact two prose romances, Lyly's *Euphues* and Sidney's *Arcadia* had given the first impulse to the expression of national pride through a literature devoted to beauty. Both these works are mannered and artificial in their symmetries and decorations, and this characteristic persists throughout the age, only being transcended in the great (and numerous) works where the sweep of passion, rhetoric, and imagination carries them along on the flood. In the many anthologies, collections of shorter poems, and in the madrigal texts and lute-songs, these artifices are prevalent, but they have their own pleasant flavour when matched with the current musical convention of playfully intricate counterpoint. The texts chosen for music demand simple and obvious emotions, suitable for development one at a time, and they depend on their musical setting to complete the effect. But they, and their Italian counterparts of an earlier generation, belong to the story of music, not of literature.

England's golden age is usually associated with the reign of Elizabeth I, but the English Renaissance by no means lost its vitality when it lost its "fair Oriana". The poetic impulse remained active as least until the Restoration in 1660. Ben Jonson and John Donne, who set the direction for many succeeding poets, were writing before 1603; Herrick, Marvell, and Milton after 1660. The Renaissance cannot be dated as a period; it was an attitude to life and an impulse to creation which even survived the Civil War and the Puritan interregnum. But this creative urge, coming late to England, retained its force while another attitude was beginning to develop. This was a tendency to scepticism, realism, and psychological introspection. Perhaps it owed something to political disquiet, to the influence of Montaigne and of Macchiavelli; to the first stirrings of empirical science, or to Puritanical broodings on the soul and the life beyond the grave. Whatever its sources it represented a new phase of mind, one which lacked something of the confident self-assertion of the youthful Renaissance. It was a critical mood. It prompted inner questionings in essayists and poets, it whetted the appetite of satirists, it called forth the eloquence of polemical divines in sermon, tract, and treatise. But it also fortified a tendency inherent in English drama. This was to present not merely the external spectacle of human foibles and misfortunes, but to look below the surface for their origin in character.

The theatre throughout the Elizabethan age was a vital part of public life. It was open to all, groundlings and gentry alike, an audience for whom there was one common element, life and the true portrayal of its experiences. It was rooted, like all European drama, in medieval custom; it gathered resources from strolling professionals and scholarly amateurs, from farce, historical chronicle, romance, or gory tragedy. In the latter particularly the English playwrights found their medium for probing the mysteries of human destiny. They saw tragedy as an outcome of character, not pre-ordained by fate or suiting the convenience of plot. This was their great corporate achievement, and even had there been no Shakespeare, this vast and varied output of English drama would have brought to a fitting climax the all-absorbing passion of the Renaissance for the study of mankind. But in the brilliant company of Marlowe, Jonson, Dekker, Webster, Middleton, Beaumont, and Fletcher, Shakespeare stands supreme, gathering together in himself all the gifts which they, in isolation, could display. Foremost of these qualities is his unrivalled creative power. His characters, in all their varied range, live consistently, each with his own traits and his own philosophy. They are one with us; they live on this earth we know. Shakespeare rarely takes our mind beyond the present:

"Our little life is rounded with a sleep",

but within this world he illumines our thought and perception of humanity, and stirs our feelings in sympathy with its joys and sorrows as does no other artist of the Renaissance, or perhaps of any age.

SUMMARY

The term "Renaissance" does not denote a period but an attitude of mind. It is a simple conception, a zeal to explore and express the thoughts and feelings of men as individuals, but its effects were naturally as varied as the characteristics of humanity itself. In Italy it produced a matchless flowering of art and an almost pagan delight in the sensuous beauties of man's creation. In Germany, on the other hand, it fortified the mental and spiritual life; serious people, devoted to the new Protestant religion, drew more from the new resources of humanist education than from the models of ancient art. Spain, France, and England followed Italy in absorbing the principles of Classical beauty; each found her characteristic national compromise, and went on to reach her highest pinnacle in literature and drama. Throughout Europe, with the exception of countries involved in religious warfare, the new zest for a full human life created conditions favourable to art, and under this impulse, every country produced its greatest creative genius and its most widely sustained artistic effort. It was an age which glorified man, and his vision,

imagination, and artistic interpretation of all that reaches him
through the senses. It expressed his wonder at the present,
whereas the "age of faith" had shown his fear of the future and
of the unknown. In contrast to both these attitudes, the centuries
which followed the Renaissance were to be marked by intellectual
and scientific probing of man and the physical world about him.
This new attitude was itself a product of the questing spirit of
the Renaissance, but it produced little of permanent value until
the principles underlying scientific investigation were established
in the course of the 17th century. The visual arts, and the
literature of observation and imagination, had reached their
maturity in various stages between the 14th and 17th centuries.
The works of beauty which fill our churches, museums, and
public buildings were already in existence, and so were the forms
which have continued to serve in all the arts—except one. Music
has received the barest mention in these pages devoted to the
Renaissance. It is time to look at it more closely and see its
relation to the general mind of Europe.

9

Music up to 1600

FROM the earliest days of Christianity music had been the medium through which the Church's ritual was conducted and her prayers offered in ceaseless round to heaven. Through the darkest centuries of European civilization, plainsong melody had kept alive the spirit of beauty; it ran as a golden thread about which were woven ever new textures of sound, in successive stages of imaginative and technical expansion. And outside the Church, music played a part which we easily forget in these days of the printed word. It was a medium of communication in many practical ways, as well as a source of entertainment and an outlet for the emotions. Written record has preserved far less of this improvisatory activity than of the learned art of the Church, but there is evidence enough in literary references, in surviving instruments of astonishing variety, and in pictorial representations of their use, to show how music pervaded all activities of life. The war-songs of the Germanic invaders, the royal and military signals of trumpet, horn and drums, the pomp and circumstance of courts, the humbler activities of waits and town-bands, these were part of the ordinary business of life. No less vitally functional was the music associated with magic, propitiation, and fertility; the ballads and folk-songs arising out of history, legend, and life; the music for dancing, for work and for play. And drama too, a far more integral part of life than an occasional evening at the theatre, used music to aid its declamation both in Classical antiquity and in the medieval mysteries and moralities which grew out of the Church's liturgy. After spoken dialogue had taken its place, music still performed many functions in the theatre, as our Elizabethan drama testifies, in conventional signals, in pageant and dance, and above all in the emotional intensity of its lyrics. In this last function, in intensifying the communication of human experience, music had always been inseparable from the artistic mind of Europe. Whether at the popular level of mime and minstrel, or in the sophisticated art of the troubadours and of the music-makers at Renaissance courts; whether in chanting heroic epics or in accompanying the conceits of lyric poetry, music and life had been inseparable.

This enthusiasm for music continued unabated during the European Renaissance of the arts. While these were undergoing their transformation, with quickened human impulse and under Classical inspiration, the spirit of music remained as vital as it had always been. It needed no rebirth. But musical theorists, like all writers of the 16th century, were obsessed with the cult of Antiquity. They paid homage to its music although no models existed for their guidance, and they proudly imagined that contemporary composers had recaptured the spirit of the ancients. But they reduced their Classical aspirations to nonsense by ascribing the "restored perfection" of music to the great Netherlandish composers, whose polyphony was a northern creation, and the very obstacle to the development of a new Renaissance music. Here is the crux of the situation in the 16th century. Composers were alive to the thought of their day and stirred by the spirit of Antiquity, but as musicians they were masters of a technique supremely fitted to convey the moods and thoughts of religious worship, and for that very reason, designed to exclude the wider range of experiences which derive from human passion. We have seen the transformation of the European mind in painting and sculpture, in literature and drama, under the impulse to explore that wider range, and that is what we recognize as the spirit of the Renaissance. The art of music came to a wonderful flowering while that spirit was active in Europe, but only in superficial features, and in miniature forms which captured single moods and conceits did it reflect the nature of man. It is possible to speak of music in the period of the Renaissance, but it is not possible to think of "Renaissance music" as a full expression of the human mind in the art of sound.

This is not to say that music made less appeal than did the other arts. Far from it. During the 16th century, moreover, many decisive developments were occurring which led to the transformation of its language. These were, broadly, a growing use of chordal harmony with appreciation of its expressive effect in alliance with discord and chromaticism; a natural tendency for a single melodic line to become prominent (either as the highest voice or against an instrumental background), so facilitating individual instead of corporate expression; an increasing adoption of secular rhythms from popular music into cultivated art; and an organization of the miscellaneous legacy of medieval instruments in groups and families, which provided the foundation for a well-defined instrumental art. This was clearly a reinforcement of tendencies which had been present in secular music for centuries. It was an assertion of the distinctively European character in opposition to a prevailing ecclesiastical art based on Oriental melody and on polyphony which excludes all worldly elements. But these developments, which are essential for the expression of human experience took longer to come to maturity in music than in the directly representational arts. Expressive associations must gather around musical sounds before they can form part of an explicit language, and this process was far from complete until the opera of the 17th century had done its work. These inherent difficulties of the art, and the fact that almost without exception professional musicians held ecclesiastical appointments, ensured a strong persistence of tradition. As a cultivated art of fully human expression, music was in its infancy in 1600; the ancient ecclesiastical art by then had reached its summit.

The foundations of the last great phase of this sacred polyphony were laid during the early 15th century, when the conception of unified textures based on triadic harmony gradually replaced that of virtually unrelated melodies. It was a characteristically Northern art, developed almost exclusively by Netherlanders, both in the Low Countries and France, and in the service of the Renaissance courts of Italy. It began to expand with Dufay (died 1474), from the customary three-part high-voiced textures of the late Middle Ages to a lower range in the bass, and with Okeghem (c. 1430–95), to longer lengths of overlapping phrases in continuous flow. With Obrecht (1450–1505), four-part writing became the norm, melody acquired more definition through sequences and cadences, and the musical texture more homogeneity through occasional imitation (the passing of a phrase from voice to voice). With the establishment of imitation and some degree of contrast between choral groups, Josquin des Prés (c. 1440–1521) had command of a flexible technique which he applied in every current branch of music with expressive treatment of words. Prof. E. J. Dent has referred to him as the first "Whose music appeals to our modern sense of the art". His music has the power of structure and the sensuous beauty of choral sound which we admire in the great polyphonists who followed him, but it is also charged with feeling and with that significant quality in thematic material which belongs to the greater composers. Josquin, like all the polyphonists, resorted to artificialities in word-painting, or an occasional theme "manufactured" on the letters of a patron's name, but in the main body of his work he shows how convincingly the language of music was developing its powers of expression. Two more Netherlanders, Gombert (c. 1500–60) and Willaert (c. 1480 or 90–1562), enlarged the scope of vocal polyphony, the first in five- and six-part textures, the second with *cori spezzati* (separated choirs), a choral amplification of the ancient practice of antiphonal singing, especially suitable in the two organ-galleries of St. Mark's, Venice. They were followed by Orlando di Lasso (1532–94), the last of the great Netherlanders, copious, versatile, and expressive; by Palestrina (1525–94), serene both in the austerity of his moods and in the effortless mastery of his art; by the Spaniard, Victoria (1540–1613), with his warmth of religious feeling; and by the English Tudor composers, Tallis, Morley, Gibbons, and Byrd (1543–1623). The last-named, with a full measure of the rhythmic and melodic energy which marked the English composers of that age, and a technical assurance unsurpassed by any composer in Europe, had that faculty for imparting to his musical themes the quality which belongs only to genius.

The greatest artists do not live consistently on the heights. Byrd, like all his contemporaries, used plenty of the "tags" or clichés which are inseparable from polyphony, an art which makes its effect more as a total structure in sound than by the moving quality of its details. It does not depend on melody, in the sense of a tune, complete and significant in itself. Nor does each phrase need to convey a particular verbal meaning. Polyphony is not an art of direct expression, but one which intensifies religious moods which are already defined. This is so especially in the Mass where the thought appropriate to each stage of the ritual is present in the worshipper's mind. The Motet has a wider range of expression, and it was here that the personal feeling of composers could find more appropriate outlet. Dufay's Motet *Ave Regina Coelorum* is an obvious example, with a telling personal interjection of the words "have pity on thy dying Dufay", which make a striking impact on a minor chord foreign to the prevailing mode. (Ex. 1.)

From the *Ave Regina Coelorum*. Dufay (died 1474).

The artist of course has always experienced personal feeling, and the Church's music from earliest times showed the pressure of this feeling and its demand for outlet in the melismas and contours of Plainsong, in the addition of hymns and tropes to the basic liturgy, in the combining of strands of voices and instruments to add to the splendour of the ritual, and in ever-new combinations of rhythm and melody and structural artifice which show the power of intellect in association with emotion. The Church, on the other hand, has always insisted on the absolute, the universal not the personal, the merging of the individual into a whole greater than himself. The art of polyphony, throughout its history, represented a compromise between the demands of the whole and those of the individual. The conception of an all-embracing unity is reflected in the threads of the polyphonic web, which unite to make a total effect far greater than the sum of its parts. Yet the quality, the diversity, the range, the intensity within this impersonal whole are the product of personal feeling and of the genius of individual musicians, who evolved the art and who practised it with such sublime assurance in the 16th century. The art of polyphony gave musical expression to the first great phase of the European mind, that dominated by religious aspiration, and it ranks with the greatest achievements of mind in any age, whether in art or science, in reason or imagination.

But as the European mind freed itself from religious dominance it needed outlets for a wider range of human experiences, passions, and activities, and it needed new musical techniques for presenting that experience. Just as it had developed new procedures in painting, in architecture, and in literature, as a part of the human

Renaissance, it was developing also in music a language for the expression of feeling, and the elements of this language were becoming more clearly defined during the 16th century. A separate study would be required to follow the stages of this development. (Deryck Cooke has made a valuable contribution in *The Language of Music*, O.U.P., 1959, classifying examples from the late Middle Ages onward, which show how certain basic elements of musical technique have served composers for expressive purposes.) It is easy to take for granted some features of this language, and to forget that they have evolved as part of a purely European convention. They are by no means universal, but spring from our own racial character and ways of life. For instance, it has become natural for us to assume that in general, minor intervals express "sadness" and major ones "brightness". But there is no inherent emotional quality in any interval considered separately. Different degrees of tension only arise when a particular order of sounds has been accepted as normal, and departures from that norm can then convey a sense of special effect. As long as melody and polyphony were organized on the basis of several different ecclesiastical modes (for practical purposes, the six scales starting from C, D, E, F, G, A, and using only the white notes of the piano), there was no constant standard of reference. The quotations in Ex. 2 show how much our conception of tonality has acquired expressive associations since the age of plainsong.

At (a) there appears to be a naturally serene "major" melody, and at (b) one which is "minor" and almost plaintive. But the two fragments of plainsong do not imply different moods: the same words, "Holy, Lord God of Sabaoth" are common to both. Again at (c) the music might be that of a mournful folk-song, but the words are expressing eternal praise. The melodic intervals are simply those appropriate to the respective modes of the plainsong, and no major or minor implications are present. This is true also of a great amount of polyphonic music which owed its melodic contours to those of plainsong. But the habit of combining melodies brought with it an appreciation of simultaneous sounds, and the instinct of the vocal composer was the same as that of the instrumental player whose fingers struck chords from his instruments, to choose the triad, especially in its major form, as the group which appealed to him as normal. The aptness of chordal music for direct human expression and comment had always been apparent in popular and secular music, from the

Ex. 2.

(a). (Lydian mode)

San ...... ctus, San-ctus, San .... ctus Domin us De ··

·· us, Sa · : ..... ba - oth

(b). (Phrygian mode)

Sanctus, Sanctus, Sanctus Dominus De us Sa - ba - oth

(c). (Dorian mode)

In sae-cu-lum sae -- cu - li lau - - - da-bunt - - te

days of Adam de la Hale's minor lament for a lost donkey to Josquin's lively major patter about the grasshopper. It is most significant that it was also the medium for religious expression when the Protestant faith made its appeal directly to human judgment and feeling. The chorale in Germany, the Huguenot Psalter in France, the *Laudi Spirituali* in Italy, the plain settings of the English service and the anthems introduced by Tye, did not use the labyrinthine beauties of polyphony; they were mainly chordal and syllabic, because the words needed to be clearly heard and their import enhanced by the emotional effect of congregational singing. The triad in itself makes a sensuous appeal by its euphony, and the varied interplay of its major and minor, or brighter and darker forms, could lead to expressive associations as in Dufay's motet at Ex. 1. (It is noteworthy that polyphony is suspended at that moment of purely personal expression.) Add to these already rich resources of harmony the strength and tension of discord, produced by delaying one or more notes in passing from one chord to another, and also the sense of unexpectedness produced by chromaticism, a brightening

or darkening of notes in the normal scale, and it is evident
that musical resources in the 16th century were well fitted to
meet the demands of intimate human expression which is one of
the characteristics of the Renaissance. Ex. 3 shows them in use
at the opening of a well-known madrigal, "O Care, thou wilt
despatch me", by Thomas Weelkes (1608):

"O Care, thou wilt despatch me", 1608. Thomas Weelkes.

Intimate expression, but not yet the full range of human experience or of musical scope. In this respect music is quite unlike
the other arts which reached peaks of achievement during the
Renaissance which they never again attained. Music until the
17th century was closely associated with life and thought external
to itself: with religious worship and medieval drama, with
popular entertainment and the dance, with the chanting of epics
or the enhancement of lyric poetry. With each successive phase
of these extra-musical associations it developed its own particular
formal designs—it could not otherwise have artistic significance
—in the melodies of plainsong and of the sequences, the motets
of the 13th century, the isorhythmic structures of the 14th, and

finally the sectional method of the 15th- and 16th-century masses and motets, with each line of text presented in imitative counterpoint. Each convention served its age and then gave place to another, but broadly speaking, one feature was common to them all up to about 1600: the sequence of thought and its presentation were not determined primarily by musical requirements, but by the liturgy or by the religious or secular poem which existed independently of the music. The design of a motet which presented eight lines of text in eight successive sections of music was akin to that of a medieval painting or sculpture with its rows of figures filling the picture space. In each case, religious symbolism was a more powerful motive than artistic composition. Italian painters in the 15th century achieved the art of purely pictorial composition as well as the art of human expression. Musicians in the years around 1600 had gone far in developing the art of musical expression, but they had still to find the principles by which an extended musical composition can exist in its own right. Small-scale dance movements and marches, with their eight bars or so of melody, their contrasting sections and balancing repetitions had long existed, and so had symmetrical forms in which music accompanied highly wrought lyric stanzas. How was the art of music to expand beyond the miniature and the merely repetitive?

The answer for the composers of the 16th century was still to use the long interweaving lines of polyphony. Music which served popular and secular needs, whether in folk-song, town band, or courtly festivity, tended always to rhythmic definition, rhyming cadences, and balancing phrases, as far back as our records go. But the musicians who had the highest professional skill and international prestige had learnt their art in the church. The medieval supremacy of French and English ecclesiastical musicians passed in the 15th century to Burgundy and to the Netherlanders, who carried this essentially northern art to Spain and to Italy, attracted by the splendour of courts eager for artistic glory. They transformed the native song wherever they went into their elaborate contrapuntal textures, so that the French *chanson*, the German *lied*, the Italian *frottola*, acquired the same basic technique as the church motet. The result was the 16th-century *madrigal* (and the kindred polphonic *chanson* and *lied*), a triumph of sophisticated art, and an amazing compromise between the polyphonic art which closed the Middle Ages and the urge to human expression which had marked the age of the

Renaissance. Instrumental music followed the same course. That these centuries revelled in the sensuous pleasure of producing and listening to the sounds of diverse instruments is obvious from Renaissance painting and sculpture; but the form taken by the music played was for the most part that of the ecclesiastical motet, in *fantasy* and *ricercar*, in transcription of motet, air, and madrigal.

Since art rests on compromise, this extraordinary blending of old method with new feeling offers no barrier to sheer musical delight. Perhaps its very unreality is an attraction to palates jaded by the convention which ultimately established itself, both in cultivated and popular music, as the European norm. The madrigal came to popularity with the northerners Willaert and Cipriano da Rore, working in Venice; it passed into Italian hands in the mid-century with da Monte, Marenzio, Monteverdi, and Gesualdo, and to the Court and country houses of Elizabethan England, and a glowing sunset in the work of Byrd, Morley, Weelkes, Wilbye, and Gibbons. It was music associated with lyric poetry, some at a high level as in frequent settings of Petrarch, some at the average level of pastoral and amatory convention. Artificiality scarcely detracts from its value, which depends rather on the wit and verve of the music, its intricate patterns, and its enhancement of sentiment, from the wayward and charming to the borderland of true emotion. But its complaining lovers are never really the victims of tragedy. For the reflection of the larger issues of human experience in musical terms we must turn to the opera of the 17th and 18th centuries, where both the emotional content and the musical forms begin to approach the dimensions we have seen in the art and literature of the greatest figures of the Renaissance.

SUMMARY

Music permeated life in the 15th and 16th centuries and aroused the same enthusiasm as was extended to all the other arts in that period of the Renaissance. But it differed from them in being the only one which had not developed its most characteristic forms before 1600. The visual and literary arts had made a sharp break with medieval practice, and established the forms which have remained basic through all succeeding changes of detail and emphasis. Many of the greatest masters of all time in those arts had already done their work. The position was different in music because of the overriding influence of polyphony, that last great product of medieval ecclesiastical art. Yet the urge to human expression was strong. It found vent both in trivial ways—in naïve word-painting and descriptive representations of battles, bird-calls, and female chatter; and in sublime ways, through moving and beautiful songs, and through the association of expressive harmony with the moods and emotions of mankind. Before the century ended Dowland was producing his *Ayres*, players were drawing characteristic sounds from their instruments which would open up a great new world of pure music, and the first steps had been taken towards the new art of opera which was to bring the decisive break with the past. But for the 16th century polyphony was supreme. Like Gothic architecture, it sends the spirit soaring but it does not speak with simple human accents. The new forces which were to produce the new birth, the Renaissance of music, belong to the 17th century, when they brought into being the art through which the deepest emotions of man can find expression.

10

Music in the Seventeenth Century

THE division of history into periods marked by centuries or events can never be more than a convenience for study. The texture of life shows no neat patchwork design. To choose the particular year 1600, or even a score of years around it, may seem arbitrary, since many significant developments had occurred in music even before the mid-16th century. A strong sense of harmony had long been apparent despite the prestige enjoyed by polyphony; this can be seen both in the practice of composers and in scientific analysis like that of Zarlino in 1558. Empirical use of chromaticism for expressive purposes was transforming age-old habits in the blending and progressions of sounds, and the venerable tradition of the ecclesiastical modes was well on the way to disintegration. New textures abounded: in contrasting choirs, varied associations of voices and instruments, in solo melody and accompaniment; in new instrumental forms and techniques such as ricercari, airs and variations, pairs of dances like the *pavan* and *galliard*, toccatas for organ or for virginals, and in lute accompaniments and figurations which arose from the demands of fingers and not voices. A general tendency to secularization made its mark on music as on life at large. The temporary seriousness induced by Counter-Reformation discipline did not prevail for long against the temptations to courtly splendour, especially in the heyday of Venetian luxury and ostentation. The historian of musical activities may well carry his story across from the mid-16th century into the 17th; the New Oxford History of Music includes a period from 1540 to 1630 for many good reasons.

But a decisive change of outlook, and with it, a complete innovation in musical method occurred at the turn of the century. It arose from the efforts of a group of Florentine artists and musicians about the year 1580 to revive what they (wrongly) thought to be the Greek manner of presenting drama in continuous song. Vicenzo Galilei, father of the astronomer Galileo

14. The Hofhaltung, Bamberg, Bavaria. 1591.

15. The Monastery of Melk, on the Danube. Prandauer, 1702.

Galilei, gave impetus to experiments in a new style by his *Dialogo della musica antica e della moderna*, 1581, and by his association with the Florentines. He brought the thinking of this group of enthusiasts to a focus by his implacable opposition to polyphony as the chief obstacle to the clear expression of words. The method they adopted was a kind of vocal declamation called *recitativo*, with light chordal accompaniment, and it was designed to be flexibly interpreted by the singer so as to suggest the natural inflexions and rhythms of speech. This integration of drama and music came about through the scholarly aspirations of the "Camerata", as the Florentine group was called, but it quickly became the most fashionable form of entertainment both privately in courts and palaces, and in public as well, after the opening of the first opera house in Venice in 1637. It did so for several reasons. These new resources of music joined with those of the pastoral drama which absorbed the Italian mind at the close of the 16th century. Guarini's *Pastor fido* (the Faithful Shepherd) appeared in 1590 and had an astonishing vogue and influence in Europe until the social world it mirrored passed away with the French Revolution. Monteverdi's *Orfeo* of 1607 is now familiar enough for us to savour this artificial world, and at the same time to recognize the perfect aptness of music for its conventional scenes and personages. The new music was also well fitted for association with the themes of Classical mythology, through its powers of declamation and its heightening of tragic emotion. Although on the purely musical side it abandoned the resources of a mature and highly developed art, it clearly chimed with the mind of the age in its subject-matter, in its fresh illumination of Classical subjects without trace of medieval overtones. In this it was the first unadulterated expression of the Renaissance mind in music. It was naïve, but so in many ways were Giotto's frescoes, in their concentrated expression of emotion. The range of subject widened as the 17th century progressed: Monteverdi's *L'Incoronazione di Poppea*, 1642, was the first opera to deal with a historical theme, and it also included comic characters. But in spite of the initial urge to speak with the accents of nature, no art ever became more stylized than this one, which provoked Addison's raillery a hundred years later and Johnson's famous definition of it as "an exotic and irrational entertainment". These words convey the strongest of the reasons for the immediate popularity of the "nuove musiche": the age demanded splendour and lavish spectacle in its amusements and festivities, and opera provided unrivalled opportunities for the joint display of all the arts and crafts of the stage. In particular, it gave an outlet for the Italian's passionate love of singing, now uninhibited by the intellectual discipline of counterpoint. "The baroque opera is, in fact, the bridge by which the artistic emotions of Italy passed finally from architecture as a chief means of expression to music, thus calling into existence the classical school of the early 18th century in which Haydn, Mozart, and Beethoven were to learn the first principles of the sonata and the symphony." (E. J. Dent, *Alessandro Scarlatti*.)

The phrase "baroque opera" raises one more point of general significance. The early monodic experiments in musical drama were certainly a Renaissance phenomenon, both in their purely Classical inspiration and in their insistence on a new and direct form of expression. But this musical development came late, at a time when the Renaissance ideals of artistic purity in thought and style had yielded to a craving for extravagance in art as in life. Criticism has firmly tied the label "Baroque" to this phase of European experience, and the musical child of the idealist "Camerata" found itself growing up in this very age of exuberance, and quickly adopting the manners of its day. The position of music in the Renaissance is therefore a curious one. The lyric impulse found its outlet in the madrigal and kindred forms which looked back, in their technique, to the Middle Ages; the dramatic impulse was deflected for a time by superficial demands of fashion, but it was developing a language which in essentials was that of the future. It is for this reason misleading to speak of "Renaissance music" as if it occupied a clearly marked period in time. The view that the years around 1600 represent a watershed between old music and new lends itself less easily to misconceptions.

In all the arts, when the decisive break with religious and medieval traditions had once been made, the new forms which came to their classic perfection through the Renaissance impulse remained basically unchanged until the late 19th century. This is equally true of music. The decisive break with the past came with the abandonment of polyphony, and after 1600 a new convention began to take shape which lasted, in essentials, until the present century. The classic form of this musical language was not perfected in the 17th century, but all the experiments of that age of transition contributed in two broad ways to its clearer definition, the first in its power of expression, the second in its purely musical organization.

Composers of the previous century, even in their contrapuntal art, had undoubtedly shown an interest in conveying the meaning of a text, but in general they did so objectively, by external suggestion such as word-painting. But the attitude of the monodists was subjective. They were intent to communicate the feeling and not just the visual image called up by the words. They used solo declamation not only so that words could be clearly heard, but so as to give free play to individual passionate utterance. In doing so, they brought into being a new conception of melody, modelled on the inflexions and rhythms of speech, seeking tension through augmented and diminished intervals and pathos through plaintive drooping phrases. It was a mannered art and full of clichés, but it was precisely through this repetition of formulas that certain emotional connotations became attached to melodic phrases. Associations thus gathered about purely musical sounds have a way of asserting themselves when these sounds are heard again without a verbal context. Prof. E. J. Dent stressed the part played by "the subconscious memory of Italian Opera that enabled audiences to follow the thought of the symphonic composers". (*Mozart's Operas.*) Along with the new melody, harmony continued to exert its expressive influence, as it had done increasingly in the later madrigals. Like melody, it can reflect varying tensions of feeling by its varying relations to a smooth and accustomed norm. From about 1670 the tonal system of major and minor scales was firmly established as this norm, and within the system, chromaticism had a clearly defined status for obtaining colour and expressive effect. It was a synthesis of musical resources in which intellect and emotion exercised a balanced interplay. It was the language which the general musician and music-lover—corresponding to the legal conception of the "reasonable man"—recognizes as his own. In the first half of the century there was much fluidity; diatonic harmony which was neither modal nor tonal provided a background against which chromatic juxtapositions of chords could make dramatic effect. Thus Monteverdi, in his *Orfeo*, at the announcement of Eurydice's death, could produce a sudden chill of anguish by switching, in two chords, from E to C minor, which is far more telling than the constant flux of chromatic progression in the excited emotional effusions of, for instance, Gesualdo's madrigals. With Monteverdi the language of expression is more clearly defined and the musical significance therefore more lucidly communicated. The clarification of this kind of musical grammar was complete, in Italy, before the end of the century, as for instance in Alessandro Scarlatti and Corelli. Not quite so in contemporary England, where the fluidity of Purcell's progressions, subtly coloured by modal reminiscences, is one of his great attractions.

Recitativo, with its supporting chords threaded together on a continuous bass—the *basso continuo*—was the medium for narration, adaptable to all the moods of human life from high tragedy to pattering comedy. But art does not merely copy life: it weaves its experiences into patterns of its own. The lyrics in Shakespeare's plays distill the essence from a mood or situation, and it was not long before the same impulse was at work in the musical dramas of the early 17th century. Occasional transformation of realistic declamation into passages of melodic appeal produced the *arioso*, a moment of reflection or of heightened emotion sublimated to a higher musical plane. The *aria* had the same function but was on a larger scale and it had a self-contained musical structure. The chorus also added its resources, both for requirements of plot and scene, and also, like the aria, for purposes of artistic intensity and comment. Add to these features the purely instrumental introductions and interludes, and the natural contribution of dancing, especially when theatrical display is in fashion, and it is clear that music for the stage had acquired new purposes, dimensions, and forms.

It also acquired a new relationship to words. As the early monody developed into full-scale opera there was no longer any question of setting a pre-existing text, complete in its own right. There is no clearer sign of the rebirth of music than this, that a text, a "libretto", had now to be devised so that a total effect was produced in terms of music, not of literature. This musical demand asserted itself in two ways: in the overall scheme, to provide opportunities for arias, choruses, dances, as well as for dramatic narration, and in the character of the libretto for each aria or chorus. Music needs time to unfold. It takes longer to sing Handel's great conception of praise than to say the word "Hallelujah". The madrigalists, in their sophisticated art of vocal chamber-music, could make naïve or witty fleeting pictures of words in sound, but the musical dramatist must draw the full emotional implications from the mood which the word conveys. For this purpose he needs a text which does not flit rapidly from one thought or image to another, but which concentrates on a predominant emotion appropriate for broad musical treatment.* Thus, a scene from *L'Incoronazione di Poppea* which expressed the different sentiments of slighted love and desire for vengeance gave Monteverdi appropriate materials for effective musical contrast. He was a master of subtle nuance, both musical and psychological, but the general demand of the age was tending towards obvious theatrical presentation. The innumerable libretti of Italian operas for a hundred and fifty years were mostly devoid of literary merit, but their conventional themes provided the kind of basis which music needed in order to develop its own large forms. This new kind of partnership between words and music was not restricted to opera: it was characteristic of a large amount of music in that era, religious as well as secular; it served for some of the great creations of Bach and Handel as well as for a multitude of ephemeral works. It facilitated the production of music for empty displays of virtuosity, but it also provided the large composite forms in which both intellect and emotion could combine at the highest levels of art.

The new aesthetic outlook of the 17th century transformed the expressive language of music. In important matters of form, texture, and interplay of voices and instruments it contributed also to the second stream of development, that of purely musical organization. In this, it was reinforcing a tendency, in fact an urge, which had always been present in the secular music of Europe, towards clear-cut rhythms, balancing phrases and contrasting sections associated with dancing or with lyric stanzas. As long as musicians depended primarily on the church for their employment and prestige, the native strain of music was subservient to polyphony. The far-reaching changes of the 17th century were not sudden innovations; they were developments of latent resources which now for the first time received the fullest professional cultivation, and they were fruitful and permanent because they arose directly from the instincts of the European peoples. In this connexion the work of Monteverdi (1567–1643) is particularly significant. Both in his compositions and in his declared beliefs he made it clear that music was taking a new course: his *seconda prattica* had different aims from those

---

* The Italians from Galilei onwards recognized this as a new aesthetic principle; they used the word *affetto* for the prevailing emotion, or "affection", and the Germans of the early 18th century perpetuated the tradition in their *Affektenlehre*.

of the *prima prattica*, to which he paid full respect as a noble tradition of the past. As a court musician he wrote madrigals throughout his career—his eighth collection appeared in 1638— but long before the end, only the old poetic name remained; the musical language was new. Indications of the trend of his thought appeared as early as 1582 in his three-part motets, the *Cantiunculae*, and more still in the three-part *Canzonette* of 1584. The *Canzonetta*, like the *frottola* and *villanella*, was a product of the Italian popular tradition of secular song, and its simple structure, its refrains, its dance-like character, its naïve chordal progressions contrasting with the complexities of madrigalian polyphony made it a suggestive model for a composer whose instincts led him to seek clear musical means of expression. It is desirable to indicate the main features of this process of clarification, which he carried also into the five-part texture of the madrigal, since it represents not just the disintegration of a perfected art, but the foundation on which another was to rise.

First, in the character of melody. Phrases and motifs suggested by verbal rhythms, instead of crossing from voice to voice in imitative style, tended to recur in answering patterns, in sequences, and with their points of climax at metrical accents. To secure a good melodic shape, Monteverdi would change the order of words, use repetitions, make additions to the text, or run two verbal phrases together to form a longer musical whole. The bass, above all, changed its character and its function. Instead of joining in thematic interplay with the other voices, it became simply a foundation of the harmonic structure, with a broad pattern of its own. [See Ex. 4.] The simple cadential progression of alternating fifths and fourths, the descending scale, or mixtures of these steps and leaps, became fixed as clichés which embedded themselves in the music of the 17th century. But in doing so they made possible a new approach to musical structure. Repetition of the pattern, either at the same pitch or with modulation, provided a thread which the composer could extend at will. By devising fresh figurations in the upper parts and new relations with the recurring bass, he could develop long movements which have a greater unity than those consisting simply of successive unrelated sections. The basic pattern could also appear in upper parts. This technique of *ground bass, chaconne,* or *passacaglia* contributed richly to music of the

"Baroque" period (i.e. to about 1750) and to the creation of a
new type of counterpoint.

Secondly, a new view of texture emerged. The use of two
upper parts, often running in parallel thirds or sixths over a
plainly harmonic bass, gave Monteverdi a means of expression
which could scarcely be simpler. Purely as musical design, it was
a sad decline from the interwoven traceries of the 16th-century
madrigal, but it proved to be the source of a great new stream
of music, both vocal and instrumental, which brought unsurpassed beauties within the bounds of its simple convention. But
this was in the future, when melody had learnt from voice and
violin to follow smooth and attractive contours, and had, by
consistent use of germinal motives, developed a language for
conveying purely musical thought. To allow two voices (or
instrumental soloists) full scope for their melodic flights, for
dialogue or intriguing interlacings, a thin texture of accompaniment was desirable. The *continuo* bass and a light harmonic
support from the harpsichord supplied this background. The
accompanying group then proceeded to establish itself in all
instrumental textures of the "Baroque" era. It became indeed
such an inseparable element of that music that the term
"Continuo Period" has been suggested, with excellent reason, as
far more appropriate than "Baroque", which has no possible
relevance to much of the serenely beautiful music of the age.
Many of the string sonatas, for example, in this particular trio
form, exhale the pure tranquillity of the early Italian Renaissance
spirit, a fact which emphasizes the incongruity of attempts to
attribute common characteristics to all the arts and thought of
an epoch.

Thirdly, clearly defined sectional music, long familiar in
popular tradition, brought new resources of contrast and new
forms of organization into cultivated art. In his early *Canzonette*,
Monteverdi chose a poetic form which called for this balancing
of sections, and which emphasized the principle of repetition in
its refrains. His constant aim was to achieve a union between
words and music. This meant for him not merely following the
order of a text, but enhancing its effect by the power of music's
own order. It is a basic human trait to find satisfaction in statement, contrast, and recognition of a re-statement. Folk-songs,
ballads, and dances embody this principle, and as the secular
spirit prevailed increasingly in life, so did the formal principles
which underlie its expression in art. Monteverdi himself used a

variety of sectional schemes: AABB, ABB, the finally ubiquitous
ABA, the *rondo*; but no one could claim to be a sole inventor
when all the tendencies of the century were converging on a
metrical basis of music, on formal schemes within movements,
and increasingly defined conventions in combining contrasted
movements. These new forms of musical order gained sharper

Sonata on "Sancta Maria". No. XI from Monteverdi *Vespers*, 1610.

definition in proportion as the tonal system of major and minor scales superseded the more fluid progressions within the modes. The loss of freedom in basic harmonic relations has to be set against the gain in precision which the new tonal system gave to musical language.

Fourthly, developments in instrumental technique affected the structure of music. As players sought out the characteristic idioms of their instruments, they brought into being new figurations which enabled composers to give far greater individuality to motifs, which are the premisses of musical thought. Monteverdi gave prominence to the germinal idea and its function in musical logic. He, and the 17th-century instrumentalists in general, greatly extended its effectiveness through the variety and incisiveness of their rhythms and melodic patterns. Thus the short phrase A in Ex. 4 (a) imprints itself at once on our minds, and the persistent use of its short motive (a) ensures homogeneity throughout the section which it initiates. The assertively harmonic bass pattern at X and Y (which is repeated twice more) provides a ground-plan for the whole eight-bar section, but although it imposes a rather square two-bar sequential character on the texture, the interlacing entries of the violins in bar two and the cornetti in bar four serve to hide the seams. In Ex. 4 (b) a change of time and figuration in the opening phrase B makes a quite fresh impact, and gives a different character to a new eight-bar section which is otherwise basically the same as the first one. (This kind of sectional variation was common in the early 17th century, notably in the *canzona*, of which Frescobaldi was a leading exponent, where contrapuntal textures alternated with harmonic and dance-like sections in one continuous movement. From there it was only a short step to the idea of splitting the work into separate movements, a principle already existing in the pairing of slow and quick dances, and their further grouping into *suites* of several stylized dance pieces.)

The textures of Ex. 4 are only mildly instrumental; it is obvious that the choice of thematic material can be immeasurably enlarged as keyboard and string textures diverge more and more from the normal range and contours of vocal music. The sharp contrasts which they afford are valuable not only in defining thematic material but in the continuation of a thought after its first presentation. The four descending crotchets at (a) in Ex. 5 take on a new aspect at (b) and a still further intensification

Ex.4 (b)

Ex.5 From "Quia fecit" in Monteverdi's *Magnificat*, 1610.

at (c).* This is a process of musical thinking, or developing an implication from a given statement. Ex. 6, which can be heard simply as a vigorous and finely shaped melody, is something more than that: it is a masterly presentation of a thesis which Bach proceeds to develop in all its aspects, and it depends on

Opening Ritornello, Clavier Concerto in D minor. J. S. Bach.†

† Bach adapted this melody from some previous source, at present not known, but its melodic structure is typical both of his work and of his contemporaries who were writing in the Italian string tradition.

the germinal motives (see a, b, c) for the basis of its thought. A hundred years of experience in this new use of musical motifs lay between Monteverdi and Bach. In this respect the 17th century reveals a fascinating aspect of the European mind in one of its fertile constructive phases. The output of instrumental music was enormous, not much of it bearing comparison with the mature art of the 18th century either in quality of thought or attractiveness of theme, but all of it bringing the pleasure of pure and peaceful sound to the harassed ears of this present age. It was marked by persistent search for patterns which could sustain long stretches of music, but it was only in the decade or so before 1700 that the various compromises of the age—old contrapuntal forms transferred to instruments, dance movements, sectional variations, ground bass, and such patterns—gave place

* It happens that the vocal virtuosi of the Baroque age—and this kind of ornamentation is Baroque—were addicted to such roulades, but none the less, the real source of figural creativeness is found in the new instrumental techniques.

to the structural principle which was to underlie all subsequent music. This was the principle of thematic development illustrated at Ex. 6, and the composer who did most to establish it was Alessandro Scarlatti (1659–1725). He found scope for inventiveness especially in his chamber cantatas, which could evoke more intellectual response than operas designed primarily for entertainment. But the very routine of opera production ensured the growth of his technical command and the dissemination of his style and methods of structure. He soon discarded the ground bass, since melody itself, with its logic of phrase and motif, could determine the whole structural design. Melody moreover, with Scarlatti, was something more than a succession of sounds used as a basis of structure. It had, most often, the intangible quality of tunefulness, of completeness in its own right which for the average person is an indispensable attribute of melody. It is present in popular song—the old secular tradition of Europe—and it is surely not surprising that music written between 1700 and 1900 makes such a general appeal, since it has absorbed that ancient popular tradition and made tuneful melody the basis of its art.

There can be no prescription for the making of tunes, but there is no difficulty in recognizing two features which they all possess: a quality in their germinal motif which evokes emotional response, and an organization of their constituent parts which satisfies the mind. Through their fusing of intellect and emotion they make a direct communication with the listener which deeply satisfies his own dual nature. Individual responses vary with the infinite degrees of interplay between thought and feeling, in composer and listener alike. National character and tradition also exert their influence. Scarlatti's contemporary, Purcell (1659–1695), is English in his response to words, vigorous to the point of angularity, but always intense and poetic; English too in his command of counterpoint, or rhythmic and harmonic subtleties which spring from his Tudor heritage as well as from his personal genius. With him the emotion is concentrated, the intellectual play is intricate; with Scarlatti those basic qualities find outlet in larger spans of broadly flowing melody, addressed to a different audience. And Schütz (1585–1672) again is different. Combining with his own temperament and tradition such varied elements as the Venetian antiphonal choruses and much of the technique of contemporary Italian opera, he achieved his own distinctive blend and power of communication, and opened the musical mind of Germany to new possibilities of religious expression.

With lesser men we are more conscious of the many innovations of the century than of the integrating power of genius. In their work we can see the corporate mind of an age developing the forms of pure musical sound in sonatas and concertos, suites and fugues and chorale preludes for the organ. From our vantage point in time, we know the majestic creations which Bach was to erect on their foundations. But we can also be fascinated by the working of their own minds, as we are with those of the contemporary scientists who were contributing to a larger synthesis of thought. For some people indeed, works of art are separate experiences in themselves, not contributions to a larger corpus called Music or Painting. This is a perfectly valid but quite subjective approach to isolated works. It is also true that works of art belong to a corporate mind which is constantly developing its experience. Within a period, and its forms and style, there is enough common ground for observation of general characteristics and tendencies. "Art builds on art", and a succession of works will show features carried on, suggestions developed, and scope enlarged. No sensible person is likely to imagine that a work is better merely because it is bigger in size; nor is he likely to claim that a fugue of the 19th century is better than one of the 17th because it is later in time. But when he sees men working at the same problem, for instance the structural possibilities in fugue, he is observing the corporate mind at work, seeing it in a phase of its history, and realizing the scope of its ultimate achievement. He is not necessarily making aesthetic discriminations, but he is certainly accumulating experience on which aesthetic judgment can be based. Anyone who compares the fugue by Fischer (No. 247 in Vol. II of Davison and Apel's *Historical Anthology of Music*) with that in E major, Book II of the 48, by Bach, will be left in no doubt that Bach has "opened magic casements", if only through wider modulation, the subtle modification of the subject in F sharp minor, and the fascinating stretto in diminution, which were not attainable within Fischer's restricted range. This is not the same thing as judging the work of one period by the standards of another; it is comparing like with like, and it is on such grounds that great musical thinkers like Parry and Tovey made their judgments of this age. "The 17th century is, musically, almost a blank." "If all the music of the 17th century were destroyed, not a single concert-goer would miss it." A different opinion is held by some to-day, who reject the idea of evolution in the arts and refuse to regard one man's work as merely a preparation for later achievements. If emphasis is on the word "merely", there is justification for the protest, and for insisting that every work should be appreciated in terms of its contemporary thought. But to reject the principle of evolution outright is to deny all continuity of influence, to deny that later composers find both example and stimulus in the tradition they inherit. The attitude of the artist is surely expressed by Ingres: "The greatest of Nature's geniuses is not rich enough, in himself, to body forth all that he needs from his own resources. He who does not wish to draw upon the contributions of others is soon reduced, in his penury, to that most miserable form of imitation: the imitation of his own works." No composer drew more from tradition than J. S. Bach. His work and that of his contemporaries dwarfed the 17th century's, but it grew upon their foundations. It seems a poor advocacy of the earlier century to extol it for its individual creations and refuse, by a dogmatic generalization, to recognize its contribution to the future.

A summary of the musical output of this century would form a catalogue rather than a coherent picture. To name even the chief composers, to take a fleeting glance at the scenes of their activity in court, chamber, and opera-house, to envisage the purely musical problems they were solving in new textures and new forms, is to realize that a world of thought and experience invites exploration, one that no brief verbal account can illuminate. It is to realize also the spell this world can cast on those whose imagination takes them outside the walls of the average concert-hall. But in relation to the general mind of Europe, the music of the 17th century is of interest chiefly because it reflects a transition from an old world to a new, from a world of thought dominated by religion to one where the whole range of human passions and experience finds outlet in music. There was still one supreme phase of religious art to come—the musical flowering of the Reformation in Bach, and the baroque art and architecture of an age of sumptuous display—but the prevailing tone of the 17th century's music was secular. Its language was new, both in purely musical features and in the potent emotional suggestions it acquired in association with opera. By the end of the century it had assumed the form which the average person—whether musical or not—considers to be normal, and in doing so it brought to full artistic cultivation the natural musical impulses peculiar to the peoples of Europe.

11

Music and Art in the Baroque Era
1600–1750

THE musical resources which were developed primarily in opera in the 17th century proved fruitful too in all the other branches of the art. Many of the forms which have persisted in subsequent history came into being in that century: opera, oratorio, and cantata; the concerto grosso, solo concerto, and suite; the trio sonata, solo sonata, and chamber duet; and for the organ, the prelude and fugue and the numerous developments based on the German chorale. Most of these are extended forms, and many demand full resources of instruments, or ensembles of voices and instruments. They met the demands of an expansive society, interested above all in impressive spectacle and prodigal entertainment. Among the popes and cardinals, the kings and countless nobilities of that age of grandeur, there were many who depended entirely upon ostentation for their modicum of prestige; for many of them, art was secondary to virtuosity and effect. But for the artists in their service the opportunity was golden. Their activities may have been directed in particular channels, but these were broad and varied enough to give ample scope for every kind of art. And there was nothing to prevent the creative genius of the individual from soaring far above the mind of his patron. Bach wrote much of his chamber and orchestral music at Cöthen, in the service of Prince Leopold, who was a musical and discerning patron. But most of his great choral works were produced for the Lutheran services at Leipzig, and it is unlikely that his congregations could have more than a glimmering of the profundities of their great cantor's music, produced for their routine needs but wrought out of Bach's genius in devotion to his God. So it must have been with the architectural visions and triumphs of the age. Princes and prelates moved amid the splendours, but while they have been forgotten, the art which was called into being for their self-glorification exists as a permanent heritage. It provided the external environment for civilization at one of its highest peaks, and in itself was one of the great expressions of that civilized mind.

Grandiosity itself was personified in Louis XIV (reigning 1661 to 1715), in a resplendent court which existed for his glorification while draining almost the last resources from the rest of France. There was a hardness about the "grand siècle", a calculating assertion of power resting on military strength and symbolized by a court which radiated brilliance rather than warmth. While England and Holland were settling down to their bourgeois development of trade in an atmosphere of tolerance and political stability; while Spain was declining into impotence and indulging her native fantasy in art; while the numerous rulers and prelates of Italy and Germany were enjoying the amenities of life after the struggles of the Reformation, France, in the person of her monarch, was assuming the primacy in European affairs, both in politics and in the arts of life. In the court of Versailles, the French cult of "la gloire" came into being, an unwelcome spirit which has never since been exorcised in spite of vicissitudes of fortune. Transmitted in the mid-18th century to the emerging kingdom of Prussia, this appetite for power and glory was kindled in a forceful branch of the German peoples which had so far not made an impact on the life of Europe. But no portents of future developments clouded the early reign of the "roi soleil", and even at its end, when defeat and frustration followed its overweening aspirations, there was no premonition of the disaster of 1789. Throughout the age, satire and gossip, letters and memoirs sounded notes of cynicism and disillusion. Escape into the world of magic and imagination was apparent too, in the leisure writings of Charles Perrault, creator of *Cinderella* and many of the world's immortal fairy-tales; and in the dream-like world of nature conjured up in painting by Antoine Watteau (1684–1721), recalling the contemporary pastoral fashion. But for the most part, the prevailing attitude was that reflected in La Fontaine's *Fables*—that there was no reason to question the law of nature by which the world belongs to the stronger animals.

Political and social life centred on the king as roads converged upon his vast palace and gardens at Versailles. The same authoritarian spirit prevailed in art and letters. Richelieu's founding of the Académie in 1635, while stimulating literary activity, promoted regularization of the language and of poetic and dramatic practice. This was in keeping with the native tendency already

16. The Staircase, Schloss Brühl, near Bonn. Neumann, 1743-1748.

17. The Organ Gallery, Monastery Church of Neresheim, Bavaria, by Neumann. Begun in 1750.

made plain in Malherbe, and given a final polish in Boileau, a lively consciousness of the demands of style and propriety, and an unflagging zeal to discuss all matters of artistic import. In feminine salons, and in printed pamphlets, the respective merits of Italian and French, and of ancient and modern literatures were the burning topics of the day, discussions which were echoed in England, and loomed large for a century in the politics of opera in France. But if expression was disciplined, it was not cramped. The stage, from the 1630's, had become the centre of interest, and in her three great dramatists of the century France showed the power of her mind. Corneille (1606–84) was the first to reveal its particular direction, in drama concerned primarily with motive, with characters in situations which demanded resolute decisions. These were usually of a heroic nature and calculated to appeal to autocratic taste. Molière (1622–73), like Shakespeare, was himself an actor, learning his craft in the comedies of intrigue which owed much to the old farces and the *commedia dell'arte*. He brought more than a little of the medieval spirit into his humorous and satirical observation of the contemporary scene. His wit secured him the clown's licence in frankness, and his imaginative genius endowed his age, and posterity, with characters like Tartuffe, Harpagon, and Monsieur Jourdain, who are part of the background of our experience. Racine (1639–99), like Corneille, was interested in the inner nature of his characters rather than the image they presented to the world, but his concern was with their passions rather than their reflections. Under their Greek disguises, his men and women were those of his own day—those of any day—seen in the grip of their emotions. His artistry was unique, both in concentration of plot and of verbal intensity within the Alexandrine couplet, an epitome of the French literary ideal. The minor dramatists of the mid-century found a safe anchorage in the Classical tradition, and in a worship of power and heroism—in short, in "la gloire".

By the end of the century the drama was beginning to decline. Since 1673, when Quinault turned from writing comedies to his collaboration with Lully (1632–87), it had had a popular rival in opera. The French variant of this international convention had the qualities suitable for Versailles: scenic splendour of ballet and chorus, a mannered string style—the *stile francese*—of which Lully and his disciplined band were the proud creators, and a recitative adapted to eloquent declamation of the elevated language of France. The chamber art, too, of Couperin (1668–

1733) and his fellow keyboard composers bore the stamp of Gallic genius: alive to the artistic trends of the day, but rejecting all that cannot be transmuted, with nervous vitality, into precise and elegant form.

The main musical trends, however, were to be found in the courts of Italy and Germany, where composers were developing their command of instrumental resources—aided by the new perfected violin family—and contributing to a corpus of purely musical art. We can imagine the scenes of their separate activities: the numerous courts, such as the Nymphenburg Palace at Munich, where an average violinist like Abaco would contribute his sonatas to the glittering ensemble. We can recall the more consciously artistic circle of the "Academy of the Arcadians" in Rome, those meetings for performance and discussion, by amateurs and practitioners of the arts under their fanciful pastoral names—Alessandro Scarlatti as "Terpandro", Corelli as "Arcomelo", and so on—where Domenico Scarlatti and Handel made their contacts with one another and with the artistic life of Rome. The former took this background of experience with him to Spain, the latter to London, where still another mingling of strains enriched the art of music. We can turn to Venice, where Vivaldi, in charge of the music at the Conservatory of the Pietà was maintaining a standard of orchestral playing which attracted international interest and disseminated practical influence. The radiance of this instrumental art of the south penetrated to the study of J. S. Bach in Leipzig, who sent for scores and copied them, re-working them as models both for his own instruction and for the exercise of his own superior mastery.

In all this varied output of instrumental music there was a common element: the sheer enjoyment of sound. There was no attempt to express anything external to music itself. On the contrary, a mature art of organized sound had come into existence which was now independent of worship, dancing, drama, and song. Whatever its original debt to the dance, in rhythms, patterns, and forms, or to vocal textures which had found fresh development in instrumental form, music could now speak its own language with authority. Moreover, in unfolding its conceptions in sound, it was in itself a manifestation of the European mind, not merely a vehicle for communication. It was part of that phase which had opened with the Renaissance, when human experience found its most natural and significant expression in terms of art. Not that it was cultivated self-consciously

as an art; it was integrated with life, since potentates who wished
to live in the grand manner did so through the activities of their
architects, dramatists, and musicians. The sounds they heard
took the place in life which to-day is usurped by the inanities of
commercialized entertainment. Their "light music" holds its
place in our present chamber and orchestral concerts.

This pure art of sound had a counterpart in the last great
creative phase of European architecture, the Baroque and Rococo
art of the churches and palaces of Italy, Austria, and Southern
Germany. The story of this development began in the mid-
16th century, with Michelangelo's assertion of his own originality
and energy, in contrast with the serenity of the pure Renaissance.
An early landmark was the new church of the Jesuits in Rome,
called *Il Gesù*, begun by Vignola in 1568 on plans indicated by
Michelangelo. In returning to the ancient Christian ideal of a
long church leading the eye of the worshipper to the altar, it
asserted the triumph of the Counter-Reformation in Rome, and
through the Jesuits' missionary expansion it exerted an influence
far and wide over Europe. The splendour of a Renaissance dome,
with light pouring down from the windows of its drum, crowned
the junction of nave and transepts, and in its western façade,
double columns and broad volutes carried the eye with a sweep
to the central pediment. The contrast with the static poise of a
pure Renaissance building is significant: a new feeling of concentrated power emerges.

The full surge forward into the excitement of the Baroque did
not begin until the 1630's. The classical calm of the work of
Palladio showed that the spirit of the Renaissance had not yet
departed. Both in his famous book of 1570 and in his pure and
stately palaces and houses of Northern Italy, he furnished an
example which contributed elements to the classic grandeur of
France, and to the country houses of England. The central
portico and pediment was a notable feature, and so was the
opening out of buildings with side wings and colonnades so that
the house can embrace the landscape. This appealed to the age
which followed, whether in the quiet English countryside or in
the grandiose parks and ornamental gardens of palaces like
Versailles. In Inigo Jones it found an enthusiastic exponent who
brought, for the first time, the pure Italian style to England. The
break he made with the current Jacobean style, so mixed and
busy in its details, was as great as that between the new contemporary music in Italy and the old. His "Banqueting House"

in Whitehall was finished in 1622—while William Byrd was still
alive. But such building was rare in the early century; we
associate this stately and harmonious art with the post-Restora-
tion, not the Tudor world, with the London of Pepys and
Purcell, and of the other great English architect, Sir Christopher
Wren, who contributed so much to the new City which rose after
the Fire of 1666. But just as he himself was a man of many-sided
intellect, his work in architecture shows the meeting of two great
streams, the classical one we have been discussing, and the new
Baroque art which in his lifetime was transforming much of
Catholic Europe.

The Roman austerity induced by the early Counter-Reformation scarcely outlived the 16th century. By 1626 the nave and
façade of St. Peter's were completed with a magnificence which
bespeaks a changed attitude both in art and in Catholic worship.
Sheer grandeur was one aspect of the newly found confidence. It
found expression not only in cathedrals like St. Peter's and our
own familiar St. Paul's, or the great new Jesuit churches springing up through Europe; but also in monastery and pilgrimage
churches, of which Melk, with its towering position above the
Danube is a supreme example. (Plate 15.) Expansiveness and
ostentatious rivalry brought fantastic palaces into being, incon-
ceivable as dwelling-places by any modern standards of convenience, but monuments of a resplendent social life. The
Barberini Palace in Rome, begun in 1628, showed this in its
structure, its open loggia inviting public view of a life no longer
lived in the seclusion of a central court. Vienna, Salzburg, Prague,
Dresden, Berlin, Versailles—names inextricably bound up with
the life and work of composers—followed the lead of Rome.
External pomp was the ruling motive. In Germany, the staircase
itself became the focus of the building, as in the great palaces
built by Neumann at Würzburg, or Brühl. (Plate 16.) They
speak eloquently of a life of stately magnificence and of the
architects' imaginative response to its demands. In such surroundings, grandiose or elegant, heavily or exquisitely decorated,
with the dress and ceremonial which imagination brings to mind,
the music of the 17th and 18th centuries was performed.

Imposing size was not the only mark of the Baroque. Severity
and restraint in form gave place increasingly to softer and more
sensuous lines. The oval, the curved line (especially the compound convex-concave-convex), as seen in Plate 17, and interweaving patterns, became distinctive. Here in fact is a more

characteristic feature than size itself. The sense of exhilarating movement, of actual life in the building itself conveyed the mood of the age by sweeping and grandiloquent gestures. This feeling of activity acquired at times a dramatic and even theatrical intensity. In the church of S. Vittoria, Rome, Bernini's sculptural altar-group above the altar, portraying the dream of St. Theresa, her heart pierced by an angel while her anguished spirit soars on clouds to heaven, lacks nothing in emotional eloquence. But the Baroque goes further than that: optical illusion is also brought to bear to enhance the effect, as a flood of light from a hidden window plays upon the sculpture and the gilded rods which gleam as heavenly rays. A similar concealed illumination gives dramatic effect to the silver figure of St. George in the monastery church of Weltenburg, riding towards us out of a radiant light. He is shown in Plate 18, where twisted columns also appear, rising to a broken pediment with figures superimposed, breaking the structural lines and obscuring the step from the world of reality to that of illusion.

Above the Weltenburg altar in Plate 18 a corner of the ceiling-painting is visible; it is not easily distinguishable from the figures surmounting the altar pediment. Here is another pointer to the aim of these artists, to create an ensemble of architecture, sculpture, stucco decoration, and painting which makes its effect as a whole. Angels, cherubs, and saints live an active life on wall and ceiling as though they were inhabiting the building. The ceiling of the Gesù church in Rome, painted by Gaulli between 1670 and 1683 is a particularly dramatic example, where the roof seems to open and reveal the dazzling splendour of heaven, with the elect basking in glory and the damned falling, far beyond the frame of the picture panel, down the barrel-vault into the church. A similar wealth of decorative, scenic, and narrative detail was lavished on palaces and garden pavilions. The men who filled the Baroque interiors with animated forms evolved a stock of motives and developed a style which has a recognizable unity. Yet there was room for individuality, as can be seen in the endless variations of the stuccoist Feuchtmayr, in the sweep and vigour of the Venetian painter Tiepolo, or in the stillness and grace of Watteau.

Underlying the whole of this art was the genius of architects like Hildebrandt, Fischer, Prandauer, Schlüter, and above all, Balthasar Neumann (1687–1753). In the span of Neumann's lifetime a wealth of unique buildings arose in Germany which fifty years before had been desolated by continuous mercenary war. With their frank indulgence in virtuosity, and almost sculptural modelling of walls in living curves, they produced a style which can offend the purist's taste. But they could turn their art to the highest imaginative use in forms giving pure artistic delight. The oval, as a single motive, may be a source of graceful charm, in the plans of salons and churches and in ceiling decoration; or it may be multiplied in various combinations with itself. Neumann's plan of the pilgrimage church of Vierzehn-Heiligen, in northern Bavaria, shows ovals in intricate relationships with one another and with circles which form the transepts:

Vierzehn-Heiligen, plan.

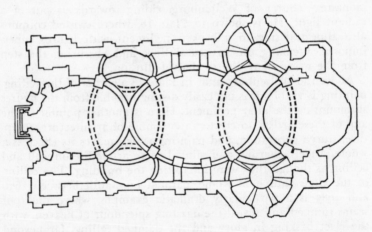

It has the fascination of a contrapuntal musical score; like a Bach fugue it reveals ever-new aspects, both in the study of its structure and in its visual (or aural) effect. To anyone standing in the building it does not easily give up its secrets; it suggests rather than reveals the lines of its plan. They are there—as in Bach—for the person who knows what he is seeking, but they do not obtrude upon the mind if we wish to abandon ourselves to the sweep of curves or be absorbed in enticing details. Plates 19 and 20 give a glimpse of some features of this architectural counterpoint. There can be no doubt that with Neumann, as with Bach, creative genius was ranging far beyond the minds of local patrons of the day.

It must not be supposed that there was any direct relationship between the art of Neumann and that of Bach. They belonged to totally different social worlds, the former to the fashionable life of courts, the latter to the organ-loft of a provincial town, and to churches which were Gothic rather than Baroque. While Neumann, with his fellow artists, was creating the architectural environment for the still evolving civilization of the 18th century, Bach was bringing an old era to its close. What they possessed in common was the mastery of the pure forms of their respective arts. Where they differed was in the application of their art. Bach gathered resources from both past and present: the recitative, aria, cantata and oratorio, the forms and textures of chamber and orchestral music from a still creative Italy; the legacy of instrumental and vocal counterpoint in the tradition of Frescobaldi and Schütz; the organ and keyboard styles from both north and south; above all, the framework of the Lutheran service and the inspiration of the German chorale, motet, and passion music. He brought them to a synthesis in his choral works, which represent a consummation of the Reformation in music. Both in that field and in his instrumental writing he revealed the finest qualities of the northern mind—its serious moral purpose, its urge to explore all the possibilities of a medium, and its intellectual power in organizing complicated details. More still, he revealed the depth of his own human insight and sympathy, which, finding expression through an unrivalled musical gift, opened vistas to the European mind which have never before or since been imagined.

We must take leave of this world which has both the vividness and the unreality of a fairy-tale. Its architecture, music, and literature remain with us, but as a way of life it belongs to the past. Although only two centuries separate it from the present day, that life, in most of Europe, still revolved about two ancient institutions, the Church and absolutist rule. But new ideas were taking shape, just as in the closing years of the Middle Ages, when old and new existed side by side in different parts of Europe. The Protestant countries of the north, where freedom of belief had fostered self-reliance in thought and conduct, were the first to evolve the compromise which led to the modern conception of democracy. The transition was not so gradual elsewhere, but after the political thinking of the 18th century and the events of 1789 had done their work there was no place in the world for the kind of society which had surrounded itself with the extravagances of the Baroque. There is a striking illustration of the effect which the democratic compromise has on art. The Place de l'Étoile, which is now included in the city of Paris, was laid out in the spacious age of Louis XIV. When Sir Christopher Wren submitted his plans for the rebuilding of London after the fire of 1666, he proposed long wide streets intersecting in star-shaped junctions like those of l'Étoile. Whether Louis XIV could have imposed such a far-reaching plan on the merchants of the City of London is an interesting speculation: the medieval plan of the City persists. And in its narrow streets, Wren's churches and his great St. Paul's, with their own compromise between Classical and Baroque, took their place in the heart of the commercial metropolis; Pepys passed busily between office and music-making and social gossip; and Purcell breathed his native genius into fashionable forms from abroad. Scientists, philosophers, divines pursued their separate quests for truth, while the Restoration dramatists made scintillating play on the scandal and libertinage of the day. But most amazing of all compromises was the absorption of Handel into the domestic life of England, the Handel who had shone in the brilliant circle of the Arcadians in Rome, master of the music of courts, but finding beneath the surface of our oddly assorted Georgian society a warm humanity which was closely akin to his own, and creating through this sympathy a music which holds its place in concert hall and cathedral and the humblest chapels in the land.

12

Foundations of the Modern World

THE major periods of history reveal their character by a prevailing attitude of mind more than by their particular personages and events. In the Middle Ages—the "Age of Faith"—we recognize the dominance of religious belief; the medieval mind sought truth in a world beyond the present. The men of the Renaissance, on the contrary, strove to develop their whole personality here on earth. By artistic vision, not by faith, they translated the chaos of temporal experiences into a world of beauty which is eternal. The difference in aim and emphasis is unmistakable. Nevertheless, in sharing a large common background of traditional lore and inaccurate knowledge, both these ages are far removed from our present world of thought. The Renaissance made a sharp break with the religious authoritarianism of the Middle Ages, but in many respects it simply substituted the authority of Classical antiquity by turning to it so assiduously for inspiration. Although it made many former beliefs untenable, it did not eradicate all the fears and superstitions which had clouded the medieval mind; many of these persisted, as did witch-hunting and quasi-magical pursuit of alchemy and astrology, almost up to the 18th century. Its literature, like that of the Middle Ages, is full of references to the pseudo-science of antiquity, with its basic elements of earth, air, fire, and water, and its neatly systematized planetary arrangements. In these respects the Renaissance looked backward; but also, by quickening the human spirit, it aided the development of those faculties of mind which are characteristic of the modern world.

What are these characteristics? With our present dependence on machines and technological processes we are not likely to underestimate the part played by science in determining the modern outlook. Its universal application to the mere mechanisms of our existence tends to obscure its true function, as an attitude to life, an inquiry into the nature of the physical world which we inhabit. It is really part of a larger inquiry still, into the nature of man himself and his relation to his environment.

It continues the endless search for truth, which the Middle Ages conducted with awe and fear of the unknown, the Renaissance with wonder and delight in the sensuous world, and modern man with purely intellectual observation of that world's phenomena.

To-day, the enormously widened field of knowledge has made specialization inevitable. We are familiar with the idea of separate branches of science where formerly the educated man could survey the whole field of "natural philosophy" with an enviable breadth of view. We seek truth therefore by means of separate investigations—astronomy, physics, biology, psychology, and so on—and as far as each branch of study is concerned, we seek it with objectivity. Science eliminates the individual as a person who knows, and is concerned only with a world of "objects". It is the function of philosophy to find what relation is possible between a knower—the subject—and the thing known —the object. It has been characteristic of philosophers from ancient times until the present, to attempt to state this possible relationship in verbal form, depending on logic for their method. But language is only an approximate form of expression, as anyone finds if he attempts to describe, for instance, a mood or a piece of music in words. Scientists, and latterly philosophers, have adopted mathematics as the form in which they record their findings, and as a means for expressing relationships. In this, they reveal the quality which we recognize as essentially modern: a purely intellectual search for truth without personal or preconceived ideas.

It was during the 17th century that this attitude became established. New theories in dynamics and astronomy showed a striking contrast with all former ideas. Copernicus, in the previous century, had challenged the medieval belief that the earth was the centre of the universe, but even so he was not free from illusions which had been fostered by Greek assumptions about a symmetrical and circular arrangement of the heavens. The successive steps from Copernicus' great initiative to Newton's formulation of the mathematical laws of planetary movement in 1687 illustrate the new approach to knowledge by purely scientific method. On the basis of Tycho Brahe's catalogue of star positions, Kepler (1571–1630) discovered three laws of planetary motion—their elliptical orbits, their varying velocity according to their distance from the sun, and a mathematical formula which described the interrelations of all the planets and the sun.

The work in dynamics of Galileo (1564–1642) made another contribution to this particular scientific edifice. As against the traditional view which postulated a "prime-mover" to initiate and maintain all movement, he held that a moving body, if left alone, will continue to move in a straight line with uniform velocity. Any change in speed or direction of movement can only be the result of the operation of a "force". On the basis of his predecessors' work, Sir Isaac Newton (1642–1727) achieved the synthesis which remained unquestioned until Einstein's work in the present century transformed all thinking about astronomy. Newton proved mathematically that all the movements of the heavens can be described by one universal law of gravitation, that is, by a constant deflection of bodies from the straight and continuous motion which Galileo had shown to be their natural property.

This collective achievement is typical of all modern scientific approach. It begins by ignoring assumptions, however hallowed by tradition. It rests on accurate observation and classification; it moves forward by the imaginative conception of hypotheses, which stand or fall by the test of experiment, and it records its progress and results not in words, but in the precise language of mathematics.

From the beginning of the 17th century, invention of instruments and improvement of method proceeded rapidly. The compound microscope, the telescope, thermometer, barometer, and air-pump assisted accurate observation, and logarithms, co-ordinate geometry, and above all the calculus made their invaluable contributions to mathematics. Pioneering work on bacteria, Vesalius' work in anatomy, and Harvey's discovery of the circulation of the blood in 1628 laid the foundations of modern medicine, and established the fact that the same physical laws apply to the human body as to the rest of nature. The writings of Sir Francis Bacon (1561–1626) helped to give direction to scientific thought, especially by their emphasis on systematic procedure and on the use of the inductive method, i.e. the search for knowledge by experiment, not by logical deduction from preconceived ideas. By the end of the century, this practical aim, to understand the forces of nature and to replace confusion by order, had created an outlook on life which was completely new to Europe. The 18th century inherited a scientific system which had reached a phase of stability, and gave grounds for much complacency about the powers of the human mind. At the same time, it derived comfort from certain systems of philosophic thought which assumed the beneficent co-operation of a deity in maintaining their well-ordered civilization.

The philosophers, unlike the scientists, could not conduct their work in specialized fields of study. In order to find man's place in the universe they felt obliged to construct comprehensive systems of thought to account for all his relationships with a larger whole. Being themselves a part of the view they were surveying, it is not surprising that they met some difficulties in matters of perspective. Successive thinkers disagreed, sometimes in subsidiary detail, sometimes in their whole conception. System replaced system for more than two hundred years. Philosophy, in its reliance on purely verbal logic, did not rest on the same foundations as science. Men like Descartes, Leibniz, and Locke received an education still rooted in the traditions of scholasticism. Although they and their successors differed from the medieval theologians in not using logic to support a previously held belief, they shared with them the conviction that they could find, by purely logical construction, the possible relations between a knowing human mind and its surrounding world of experiences. Even if their logic were faultless, their attempts to build all-embracing systems were foredoomed to failure because their theories were based on deficient knowledge of many physical processes of human perception. Their ignoring of these processes caused them to assume that no link could exist between human minds and external matter. To find a logical connexion therefore between mind and matter they made a further assumption that a higher being must be postulated who could embrace all mind and matter. These two assumptions underlay all philosophic thought until the later 19th century, when psychological study was placed on a scientific basis and threw light on the many channels by which perception of external phenomena is possible.

It may seem reasonable therefore to question the value of the philosophers' efforts. Not one of their systems ever proved permanently acceptable, and none made more than a slight contribution to a permanent body of thought. But each helped to influence the mental climate of its own age, and perhaps a continuity may be seen in the criticism which each philosopher brought to bear on the work of his predecessors. Descartes (1596–1650) is regarded as the founder of modern philosophy; he formulated its problems, and his attitude provides the key to subsequent thought. It is that of critical doubt, and this is the element which is of permanent value in his and his successors' search for truth. The determination to reject what is ill-founded or not logically tenable has become a quality of the post-Renaissance mind. Descartes threw a penetrating light on the narrow basis of human certainty with his well-known phrase *"cogito ergo sum"*. "I think, therefore I exist"; this is the one thing which he could hold to be sure amid the changing aspects of the material world. He adopted a mechanistic view of that world, a belief in unalterable natural processes, which contributed greatly to the rationalistic attitude of the succeeding age. But the gap between the "I" and the external world remained for him unbridgeable without the supposition of a God who synchronized awareness within the individual mind with every event outside it. Spinoza (1634–77) accepted Descartes' deterministic view of all physical things, but in place of the separate worlds of mind and matter he conceived experience, throughout eternity, to be a unity. In its totality it is God or nature, of which individual souls are simply aspects. Unlike Descartes and the philosophers who regarded God as a self-subsistent omnipotent being, Spinoza accepted the mental and the material and the divine together, and within this synthesis he conceived the real object of self-seeking to be to "know God" (an enlightened "self-interest" we should call it), or to aspire towards a harmonious whole. The ethical ideal is of the highest order; the whole system however is constructed by logical syllogisms and does not rest on facts discovered by observation. Leibniz (1646–1716), in the writings he published during his lifetime, accepted the reality of individual souls, or "monads", which are quite unconnected with one another; "windowless" he called them. He denied the reality of matter, and resorted to the Cartesian device of two parallel worlds which were given a pre-established harmony by a Creator. But he held very different views in his private writings, which were not published until the 19th century. In these, he found no need for a God; pure logic can determine what exists. His separate monads, too, agreeing only because each mirrors the universe from its own point of view, have no interaction: everything that happens to them is the result of their predetermined nature. This was clearly incompatible with the Christian doctrine of sin and free-will, and Leibniz thought it inadvisable to make public admission of such views.

The thought of John Locke (1632–1704) in England was more in harmony with orthodox belief in a deity, and with the "common-sense" view of reality. He accepts the existence of an external material world, but he does not accept the notion of a prearranged harmony between this external world and the individual mind. The latter has certain powers, and it can perceive through the mediation of "ideas". These are of two kinds: "ideas of sensation"—induced by sensible objects, of which the ideas are copies; and "ideas of reflection"—resulting from thought about ideas of sensation. The mind also combines simple ideas into complex ones. Locke takes over some assumptions from his predecessors, about our own existence, and about our creation by a God, but in his theory about perception he was advancing a completely new doctrine. In his day, the mind was believed to possess innate knowledge and predispositions implanted by God; Locke, in considering that it acquired knowledge only by experience, was stripping it of much scholastic overgrowth and verbal complication. He was the founder of "empirical philosophy", and of the liberal tradition of thought which was prominent in England, especially in the 19th century, and influential in France in the 18th century. Bishop Berkeley (1685–1753) did not agree with Locke that the mind can receive "ideas of sensation" from the material world. For him, an idea could only resemble an idea, and so the mind could not in itself be aware of a material world which causes sensation. He rejected the substantiality of matter. In order to explain the connexions existing between ideas in our mind, he maintained that God (the only reality) created all minds and arranged all ideas in certain sequences for us to apprehend. When Dr. Johnson reacted to this conception by kicking a stone and saying: "I refute it thus", the idealist Bishop would no doubt reflect that this very action had existed from time immemorial in the bosom of God. David Hume (1711–76) carried the thought of Locke and Berkeley to a logical conclusion which involves complete scepticism. He showed that Berkeley's arguments for rejecting material substance and causality applied equally well against assuming mental substances and causality. All alleged knowledge rested on no firmer foundation than probability. Twice two may make four a great many times, but reasoning cannot assure us that this succession of experiences will always continue. Causality is no more than habitual association.

It appears then that by the mid-18th century, the philosophers, like the scientists, had reached a plateau where they could rest after the toils of the ascent. Problems of thought and of belief did not press urgently on the mind. Although the philosophers placed reliance on the all-embracing mind of a deity, they gave no suggestion, as in the past, that faith is necessary to salvation. Their systems are interesting, on the contrary, as intellectual creations by men of genius, against a sober background of knowledge and belief. In this light, they can be studied, just as works of art can be enjoyed, simply in their own right. But at the same time they did contribute, by their cumulative effect, to a mental outlook which was tranquil and assured of a comfortable ordering of the universe both on philosophical and scientific grounds. Within this framework of thought, a great civilization came into being in the 18th century.

A further defining feature of the modern age is apparent in the broadened base of intellectual and cultural life, within a democratic framework. We take for granted in Europe and America to-day the steady pressure of a people's will, both in the election of governments and in the continuous expression of public opinion. This makes itself felt not only in politics and the external organization of life, but in all forms of thought and art. It has substituted a new patronage for the old, one which includes many different tastes and many different levels of thought. This may seem to be no more than a natural broadening of interest which has accompanied the growth of populations and the general spread of literacy. But if we think of the place of art in the three broad phases of history indicated at the beginning of this chapter, we shall find there is quite a different emphasis in the third, our present phase. In the age of faith, the arts were serving the Church, they were dominated by its thought, and dependent on its resources. In lesser degree they reflected feudal secular life, but in both cases there was a powerful unifying motive. In the age which opened with the Renaissance, the central theme was man—a variable subject indeed—but that very emphasis on man, extending as it did to the assertion of the personal rights of rulers, tended mainly to the use of the arts as a contribution to their fame and glory. Patrons differed as individuals, but they were alike in seeing art as an adjunct of power. The strand of Christian observance ran through this age as well, but we have already seen the extent to which the Catholic Church loaded itself with the pomp of courts and shared the same desire for splendour. Protestant worship did not show this attitude, but in its own environment it supplied the basis upon which an art such as Bach's could arise. In both these ages, art was closely integrated with life. It found both inspiration and active patronage through a prevailing motive in society. The power of the motive is evident in the fact that new works were constantly created in response to a living demand. They were not presented in "programmes" selected from the repertory of the past.

But where do we find a unity of purpose in the art of our own age? Is it inspired by religious belief? Is it fostered by governments, or to any great extent by the industrial and commercial concerns which are the modern forms of power? We shall look in vain for any overriding motive in our corporate society which calls art into being. We shall certainly look in vain for the funds which society in the past found it natural to expend on its way of life. In the case of music, there is no dearth of activity; endless streams of sound pour out from our radios. They run in three main channels, one of art, one of entertainment, and one of religious worship. The third is a stream which has run continuously through history, and it does not affect the present analysis. The other two follow almost entirely separate courses, and for the present we may also disregard the stream of entertainment: that has always existed at a popular level however its character has changed. In serious music, we meet a situation which has developed during the last century and a half: some is freshly composed, but most is drawn from the past, and reflects the minds of earlier ages and individuals. There is no unity, except in the tradition of the art itself, no integration with the general mind of our own age. There is, on the other hand, an incessant demand of the most varied kind, from groups and individuals, for the experience which art provides. It is almost entirely a personal one; as far as society as a whole is concerned, art is incidental.

This shift of emphasis reflects the altered pattern of political life. When rulers could take for granted their hereditary right to govern they were tempted all too naturally to neglect the practical sources of power, and to compete for prestige by the splendour of their courts. But to-day, when governments consider that their own, and their nation's, survival depends on material and military resources, they look to science and practical education to provide the basis of their power. In the last three centuries, as the seafaring nations of the north and west have turned their

18. The Altar, Weltenburg. 1718–1721. By the Asam brothers.

19. Vierzehn-Heiligen, Bavaria. Neumann. 1742–1747.

energies outward from their local seas, commercial and colonial rivalry has been a more powerful motive than the earlier ones of dynasties and creeds. It has led to wars, but it has encouraged a preference for peace. It has also stimulated thought about the political conditions most likely to ensure uninterrupted industry and commerce. The *De jure pacis et belli* of Grotius, published in Holland in 1625, first envisaged the modern science of international law, and Locke's second *Treatise on Government* of 1690, besides rebutting the idea of the divine right of kings, discussed the principles upon which a democratic community should rest. Ideas of a hypothetical "state of nature", and a "social contract", later to be charged with emotion by Rousseau, were prominent in his thinking. With Locke, respect for property was never wanting, a feature which persisted in subsequent English political philosophy, and which was congenial to a nation increasingly engaged in commerce. More potent in influencing European thought was his exposition of the principle (already established in English practice) that the making and the enforcing of laws should not be in the same hands. This separation of the legislative and the executive functions appealed with particular force to visiting Frenchmen like Montesquieu and Voltaire in the early 18th century. Through their writings, it contributed to liberal thought in France, and to the elaborate checks and balances built into the American Constitution later in the century.

"L'état c'est moi" is a political philosophy which inevitably provokes reaction. Critical thought in France found plenty of outlet in circles about the Court—La Rochefoucault, La Bruyère, de Fénelon, were eloquent in condemnation of luxury and corruption. Drama, novel, and satire contributed to the literature of protest, which came to its emotional climax in the sentimental theorizings of Rousseau (1712–78). It is easier to destroy than to build, and Rousseau's claim, in the *Contrat Social*, that the people, being sovereign, can break their contract if the state is found wanting, became a part of revolutionary thought. The poison of disruptive envy which he injected has never since lost its virulence.

But more constant than Rousseau's shallow and illusory visions, a clearer light was being kindled by which Europe was to seek its way from the rule of despotism, benevolent or otherwise, to self-reliant democracy. As kings were destined to resign their

rule, their functions were to devolve upon men whose compe-
tence in affairs fitted them for responsibility, the men of the
middle classes who had developed both character and substance
in pursuit of their professions, business, and trade. They had
also acquired a fund of technical knowledge and a lively desire
to know all the implications of the new science which was transforming thought. By the early 18th century, many of our present
methods of disseminating knowledge and artistic enjoyment were
firmly established. Learned bodies like the Royal Society in
England, founded in 1660, and similar institutions in France
and Italy, furthered the advance of pure science, while a succession of popular writers from Pierre Bayle and de Fontenelle
to Diderot and his fellow contributors to the Encyclopédie, which
appeared in France from 1751 to 1777, aimed to interpret the
whole of knowledge and bring it within the reach of any educated
person. The appearance of public concerts in England and
France, singing societies in Germany, and opera-houses throughout Europe was a sign of a similar extension of interest and
patronage in music. Painters too, especially in the north, like
Franz Hals and Rembrandt, had come to depend on a buying
public instead of court commissions and appointments. Most
potent of all influences on the public mind were the new maga-
zines, beginning with Steele's *Tatler* in 1709 and Addison's
Spectator in 1711, and followed by a spate of similar periodicals
in Germany. The resuscitation of active mental life in that
country after the desolation of the Thirty Years War contributed
a new phase of creative activity in Europe. It took its direction
from France, up to the mid-18th century, from the formulated
classicism of Boileau (which was echoed in England by Dryden
and Pope) and was applied to musical instruction and criticism
in the periodicals and pamphlets of Mattheson, Telemann,
Marpurg, and many other writers, critics, and musicians. Bach's
satirical cantata *Phoebus and Pan* is an echo of this phase; it is
the musician's reply to Scheibe, an apostle of the new taste for
whom Bach was already living in a world that was utterly
remote.

The pre-eminence accorded to reason, clarity, and formal order
in this half-century is witnessed by such terms as the "Enlightenment", the "Aufklärung", the "Augustan Age", which are applied
to the period. The prevailing tone was one of serene confidence
in the powers of reason and science, and a belief in progress and
the perfectibility of man. But a warmer stream of sentiment was

present too, a natural expression of human feeling as the middle classes became more articulate. Bourgeois subjects and moralizing tendencies in novel and play (where the dandified fop replaces the merchant as the butt of humour); an advocacy of warmer human affection as the impulses to altruism in place of the prevailing utilitarian ethics (notably by Shaftesbury in England, followed by Vauvenargues and Rousseau in France, and apparent in the ideals of Freemasonry which had a vogue during the century); the appearance of poetry and novels inspired by nature and contemplation (Thomson, Gray, and Collins, Bernardin de St. Pierre's *Paul et Virginie* and Rousseau's *Nouvelle Héloïse*); these are some of the signs of a less mechanistic attitude, which tempered the general coolness of the rational spirit. As indications of spontaneous feeling, they are more significant to us today, with our increased awareness of the deep emotional springs of human conduct, than they were to the complacent mind of their own age. The reality of emotional forces was to appear startlingly enough both in the Revolution and in the Romantic movement when the pendulum swung over at the end of the century. From that time onwards, both attitudes, one mainly practical and rational, the other idealistic and impulsive, have been apparent, both in the practical affairs and in the thought and art of Europe. This is to be expected in democratic societies which express, however incompletely, the corporate will of separate individuals. For most of the 18th century in continental Europe, the individual was still politically a cipher, and autocratic power persisted in a state of virtual inertia. In much of the art of the century it is possible to see a similar incompatibility between personal emotional impulse and accepted formal convention. But in one art, after the mid-century, there occurred one of the classic moments when mind and emotion are working in perfect fusion. It is not without reason that the music of Haydn, Mozart, Beethoven, and Schubert has remained, for the "reasonable man", that which is closest to his mind and his heart.

13

The Age of Haydn and Mozart

1750–91

ALTHOUGH new ideas and currents of feeling were spreading so widely during the 18th century, they had no practical effect on the conduct of life in the numerous courts of Europe. Even in France, up to the cataclysm of 1789, no one imagined that revolutionary armies would so soon be ranging far and wide from that very centre of civilization. The continuity of the old régime, whether at Versailles or in the remotest principalities, was still assumed to be part of the natural order, and the right to exercise personal rule was never called in question. External splendour remained the symbol of ruling power, and, although styles and fashions might change, artists still exercised their functions as the servants of princes. Geiringer, in his *Haydn: a creative life in music*, quotes a typical advertisement which appeared in Vienna in 1789: "Wanted by nobleman, a servant who plays the violin well", and the subservient position of court musicians is a commonplace of history. At the same time, patrons were in many cases both knowledgeable and appreciative. According to Reichardt, court conductor at Vienna: "The court made music with passion, and the Austrian nobility was perhaps the most musical that ever existed." Having attained the security and opportunity provided by a court establishment, an artist, speaking generally, could find plenty of scope for his talents. Haydn, who directed Prince Esterhazy's music for thirty fruitful years, provides the perfect example of this "creative life in music" satisfying both the patron's wants and the composer's impulsion to create. And since this way of cultivating music was so widespread, it determined the character of the art as a whole. All the composers and performers who created what we now call classical music held appointments at courts or depended on commissions in court circles. (The career of Mozart presents the strange anomaly of one who surpassed all others in genius but held only insignificant appointments. This arose from his own temperament, and we can scarcely regret, except for his own personal frustrations, the circumstances which made him range so widely and which therefore contributed to the all-embracing nature of his work. The fact remains that the bulk of his music was produced for courts, and through commissions secured in aristocratic circles.)

Opera, and instrumental music for diversion, continued to hold a central position in this social world, and to make first demand on the service of musicians. There was thus a continuity of musical experience which is too easily overlooked when periods are labelled "Baroque" and "Classical", and forms like "aria" and "sonata" are discussed in isolation. It is true that the classical sonata of the last quarter of the century is different in character from the sonatas in vogue in the first quarter. The intervening years produced momentous changes, but they took place within the social and the musical tradition which became defined in the early 17th century. They had, for their background, the architectural environment of Baroque art and of its later, Rococo, phase, which spread from France in the 1720's. The tone of life was predominantly secular. The moral ideals of Freemasonry were more congenial to the rationalist mind than mystical experience or institutional dogma. It is notable that no church of architectural significance was built after 1760.

Aristocratic patronage was not an unmixed blessing, even for those who enjoyed its advantages. Carl Philipp Emanuel Bach (1714–88), pre-eminent in his generation as keyboard player and composer, was highly esteemed by his royal master, Frederick the Great; but in his case, routine duties, far from giving opportunity for creative development, constituted a treadmill of stale and sterile convention dictated by the limited royal taste. Carl Philipp was only too ready to leave the court of Berlin when opportunity at last arose. A similar blight had descended on Italian opera, now for the most part reduced to a formula which provided a string of arias for vocal display. The story of its decadence has often been told, and of its ill-mannered audiences and out-of-tune orchestras. But it still remains true that these musical establishments, while serving a fashionable purpose, provided the means by which music gained a new vitality in the middle decades of the century. This revitalization was assisted from the outside by critical writings which upheld the new ideals of clarity and truth to nature, as against accumulated artificialities of vocal melody and stage convention. Middle-class tastes also fortified this tendency to simplification. Reaction also took practical form in parody and satire which used the current techniques of music and of the theatre to laugh empty heroics off the stage. Most significant was the new contribution which the musical genius of the peoples of south-east Europe brought both to performance and composition. Most apt too was the time at which their influence became effective, when possibilities which are latent in musical structure were about to receive decisive development. This corner of Europe contributed, through its particular musical temperament, to the synthesis which underlies the classical music of the late 18th century; to that fusion of Italian, German, and Slavonic characteristics which ensured a unique blending of mental and emotional factors in a purely musical art. Before taking up again this central thread of music it will be useful to look more closely at the external influences mentioned above.

The attitude of the writers of periodicals, treatises, and satires is readily understandable, since they took their tone from France, with her current ideals of pseudo-Classical purity. Being convinced of the value of clear and direct expression, they launched their attacks equally on the vocal extravagances of operatic virtuosos and on the "learned counterpoint" of the German composers of church and instrumental music. The Monodists, a century or more before, had also rebelled against contrapuntal complexities. In their case, they made a complete break with the past and substituted declamatory melody supported by an accompaniment depending primarily on a bass. On this foundation, the inexorable European urge to the interweaving of melodies asserted itself once more, to reach a culmination in the vocal and instrumental textures of J. S. Bach. His art, which to us is sublime and surpasses the limits of any period, seemed no more than outmoded pedantry to his younger contemporaries in the second quarter of the 18th century. They believed, like the Monodists, in direct expression; counterpoint to them was tasteless and unnatural. But the counterpoint which had developed during the 17th century—unlike the earlier polyphony—rested on harmonic foundations, and on clearly conceived progressions of chords and keys within a tonal system. It was possible to get rid of contrapuntal complications without discarding this fundamental harmonic structure. The writings of the critics produced a change of fashion, but they did not break the continuity of the basic tradition which had begun soon after 1600. Many of the early writers were composers as well as critics. Rameau in France, Mattheson and Telemann in Germany, put their principles into practice in their music. Telemann urged that "singing is the foundation of music", and chief emphasis on the new style was placed on melody with simple harmonic accompaniment.* Two trends were evident in practice, one showing a consciousness of style which could amount to artificiality; the other, a straightforward delight in natural and homely singing. On the one hand, men imbued with the ideals of the age of reason and "taste" cultivated elegant refinements which might match the delicacy of Rococo decoration. The *stil galant* which they affected in the middle forty years of the century succeeded in abjuring counterpoint; it substituted short symmetrical phrases punctuated by formal cadential clichés and ornamented by trills and superficial figuration. Their conception of nature was closer to the artificialities of pastoralism than to the actuality of life. On the other hand, the flood of popular melodies produced in the 18th century bears witness to the participation of a wider public. Writers who pleaded for simplicity and truth to nature did not neglect the obvious means of spreading their gospel. Collections of songs multiplied, both traditional and newly composed, for domestic, patriotic, and religious purposes. They were a vital part of middle-class life, especially in Austria and Germany, impressing their influence on music which was directed to this audience both unobtrusively, as part of the background of composers' experience, and directly, through their inclusion in operas and oratorios.

It is open to speculation whether the journalists exerted more valuable influence by encouraging active music-making than they did by their aesthetic theories. Besides simplicity, "truth to nature" was one of their recurring themes, and the way in which composers translated this concept into musical terms throws light on the processes of musical expression. The existence of intimate personal feeling could not be overlooked even in an age when reason so insistently claimed to rule the mind, and some composers, in what is called the *Empfindsamer Stil* (i.e. a style concerned with sentiment), tried to find the musical equivalent of the unheroic moods, of tenderness and melancholy. C. P. E. Bach

---

* In fact, a stream of purely beautiful melody had flowed serenely from the *bel canto* of the 17th century, and at moments in Lully and Purcell; it ran with grave nobility in Handel, in the masonic music of Mozart, and the solemn heroism of Beethoven.

was the leading exponent of this school, which represented a first and decidedly self-conscious stage in the purely musical unburdening of the human heart. He brought into the instrumental "galant" style resources which had gathered emotional associations from opera—fragments of recitative, slow movements akin to sentimental arias, yearning appoggiatures, and the emotional impact of syncopations and sudden changes of key and mood. This may seem naïve. It was not so to the young Haydn (1732–1809) when he first met the keyboard sonatas of Carl Philipp in 1750. It was not only for their lessons in "sonata form" that he devoured them so eagerly, but for their warmth of feeling and for the technical means by which it was communicated. Here was a new light in music. This discovery gave him an impetus, rather than a model to copy, but as his own powers developed, the inspiration of the older man was constantly renewed in him, so that the quest which had begun so consciously with the composers in the *Empfindsamer Stil* was continued by their successors with natural unselfconsciousness. It was for this that both Haydn and Beethoven acknowledged C. P. E. Bach to be "the father of us all". It was, moreover, through the continuous absorption into instrumental music of phraseology coloured with external associations that music developed its language of expression.

A similar translation of aesthetic ideals into musical practice took place in the 1760's in the serious theatre itself. Gluck (1714–87), or very probably his librettist Calzabigi, accompanied his "reform" of opera with a manifesto upholding the claims of dramatic truth—the ideal which the journalist-musicians had been advocating for more than a generation. But *Alceste* in 1762, and a series of operas up to 1779, revealed the power of music, when it is stripped of conventional trappings, to take on the overtones of genuine feeling. Through Gluck's simple sincerity, music proved to be sensitive to every mood, and in its turn to contribute to the atmosphere of the drama by the suggestive power of orchestral sound. Mozart's *Idomeneo* of 1781, although far superior in musical quality, rested on the same foundations. It reflected, especially in the use of the chorus, some influence of Gluck and of the French tradition, but it showed already the intimate union of music and life, and the spontaneous use of the expressive language which Mozart brought to perfection in the remaining ten years of his life. The ideals which writers had been propounding for half a century were realized in a way that could never have been envisaged.

The writers' criticism of Baroque grandiosity had a parallel in the lively movement of reaction on the stage. The popular spirit is always ready to ridicule pretension and pomposity, especially if imported from abroad, and Italian opera from the late 1720's was meeting both rivalry and mockery in many parts of Europe. Curiously enough, London, on the very fringe of musical Europe, made one of the liveliest of contributions with Gay's *The Beggar's Opera* in 1728. Using popular songs in parody of grand opera, and introducing social and political satire, it started a vogue in England for similar "ballad operas" which spread to Germany in the mid-century. The *Singspiel*, as the Germans called the comic opera with spoken dialogue, adopted the satirical attitude, and it was reinforced by the French *Vaudevilles*, or comedies interspersed with popular songs. Beside these lively entertainments, a new development appeared as an offshoot of serious Italian opera itself. The latter, in its stereotyped form, had relegated comic characters to the *Intermezzo* between acts. The success of Pergolesi's *La serva padrona* in 1733 as a comic intermezzo stimulated production of similar works in a genre known as *opera buffa*, which established itself as the musical medium for natural presentation of the comedy of life. Like the medieval miracle plays and the great dramas of the Renaissance, it soon brought all human types within its province, and so came closer to the actuality of ordinary life than the *opera seria* which was still primarily concerned (as for instance in Gluck's case) with Classical subjects and characters. And being free from the stilted convention by which the virtuoso singer gave his solo display and made his inevitable exit, it brought the characters into interplay in varied ensembles, giving scope both for dramatic and musical development. Through this intimate union with characters, moods, and situations, music gained countless nuances of expression, and it left behind the convention of the *Affektenlehre*, with its artificial isolation of single moods, and came to reflect the multiplicity of mind and experience which is ever present in life. Instrumental music in the mid-century was following exactly the same trend—towards forms which present contrasts of mood instead of persistent patterns of sound, and thus the two main branches of the art supported each other by their interaction. Court musicians were occupied in both alike: it is easy for us to forget that Haydn wrote eighteen operas and much incidental music for the theatre. But when we hear his symphonies, and the concertos and symphonies of Mozart, with their infinitely varied textures—their arresting opening motives, their broad song-like melodies, their fragments of instrumental solo and dialogue, now plaintive now nonchalant now reflective, their bustling little figurations alive with onward movement, and the mustering of all their forces in climaxes of activity or of emotional intensity—we are hearing a musical counterpart to the life which was made vivid on the operatic stage. Mozart (1756–91) brought this dramatic art to a perfection in the 1780's which has never been approached, in *Figaro, Don Giovanni*, and *Così fan tutte*, just as he performed, in the *Magic Flute* in 1791, the miracle of combining the noble idealism of Masonry with pantomimic farce and the ethereal charm of the supernatural within the framework of the *Singspiel*. The perfect blending of diverse elements, both in actual instrumental forces and in the myriad facets of life, appears even more clearly in his twenty-three pianoforte concertos, a form on which Mozart placed his own unique stamp. The new art of symphonic structure made its contribution, in turn, to the unfolding of musical drama on the stage. The finale of the Second Act of *Figaro* is a classic example of the sublimation of event, mood, and character into musical motives, phrases, and sections with their tonal and thematic individuality, but at the same time an organization which has an over-all symphonic unity.

Italy, the original home of this music of court and stage, was as fruitful as ever in genius, but the rôle she had filled since the middle of the 16th century as the leader of musical fashion in Europe was passing now in the eighteenth to new centres north of the Alps. Vienna was to be her successor, calling upon new regions fertile in musical talent. The Austrian Empire (the old title assumed by Charlemagne still lingering on), included through various treaties and marriage settlements races of German, Hungarian, Magyar, Czech, and Slavonic blood. Austria was a stronghold of Baroque absolutism, and these regions had long enjoyed educational benefits due to Jesuit missionary expansion. They were also rich in folk-music, incisive in melody and rhythm, and natives of these regions had—and still have—extraordinary natural gifts as instrumental players. From this environment the courts of Austria and Germany drew men into their musical service. Haydn came from the east, Mozart from the west. They were both Austrians, and their work came to be centred on Vienna. Gluck was born on the eastern borders of Germany, and was brought up and educated in Bohemia. From this country too came Johann Stamitz, and several notable horn players; from Moravia, Richter; Wanhal was born in Austria, though of Czech origin; and Austrians too were Wagenseil, Monn, Holzbauer, and Dittersdorf. Italian musicians were as active as ever in all parts of Europe, but these newcomers made the most decisive contribution to the instrumental art which was to become characteristic of the latter part of the century.

When their influence came to bear in the 1740's, vocal music was still pre-eminent, as it had been throughout European history. A great amount of music did exist which was independent of words—the instrumental works of J. S. Bach, and the sonatas and concertos of the contemporary Italian style are proof enough of this—but even so, it was in the vocal virtuosity of Italian opera that the age still found its characteristic expression. Instrumental music, in the main, provided a background for social purposes. But within fifty years there had come into existence symphonies, concertos, and string quartets of high artistic purpose, which remain permanent expressions of the European mind, of the same order as Gothic architecture, the visual arts of the Renaissance, and the imaginative creations of Dante, Cervantes, and Shakespeare. Pure music in its own right had become the highest expression of the human spirit. The musicians of the Austrian Empire contributed to this transformation with their particular talents. They were not by any means its only cause, but they influenced its character. Their genius was instrumental, whereas the Italian had been vocal.

The prime factor in this transformation was the revolt of mind against the rhetoric of all that was Baroque. In this negative spirit, the *galant* and the *Empfindsam* styles played their transitional rôles. The function of the new generation of orchestral players and composers was to set these self-conscious styles alight with the fire of music—music as sound, not as propaganda. The galant style had replaced the long unfolding lines and interweaving patterns of the art which culminated in Bach. It was in vogue when Johann Stamitz came to the Electoral Court at Mannheim, first as violinist, then as director of the chamber orchestra from 1745. He and his players, many of whom were also composers, brought a healthier vigour to its precious and ornamented manner, and they became not only the foremost ensemble in Europe, but did much to create the modern craft of orchestral playing and composition. Their particular achievement was to evolve a technique for varied expression, both in degrees of loudness and softness, and in sharply contrasted themes. Jommelli had already used gradations of sound for expressive purposes in opera. By making a regular feature of such nuances, and of arresting openings and exciting crescendos, the Mannheimers did more than merely impress their contemporaries by their virtuosity; they added a vital resource to the pure language of music. Their contribution was like that made by opera buffa to the stage, where interplay of moods and characters replaced the persisting "affekt". The new orchestral technique led naturally to the disappearance of the *basso continuo* and harpsichord fillings of the middle texture. A greater cohesion as well as variety of orchestral sound became possible as horns took their place along with the wood-wind in filling the gap between upper and lower sounds. Stiffly used at first, this new resource soon stimulated creative imagination. Textures must be composed throughout if they are to reflect the kaleidoscope of changing moods and thought which characterize symphonic art. The static performances of operatic soloists were giving place to the natural interaction of people in life; in the same way, the unrelieved sound of unvaried orchestration lasting throughout a movement was being replaced by the irridescent changes which reflect the normal experience of humanity. Tears are close to gaiety in life: Mozart could convey this, and so much else, with exquisite art—but only after the mid-century's transformation.

Along with these aesthetic and orchestral reorientations went the completion of purely musical developments in structure. The ruling principle in the great instrumental art of the Baroque age had been thematic unity. Bach develops the whole first movement of his D Minor Clavier Concerto from the germinal motives of the ritornello shown in Ex. 6. Artistic variety is ensured by their appearance in fresh keys and in sections which differ in vigour of movement or in colour of harmony. "Pattern" is a mechanical word to apply to such a living texture, but it suggests the conception of an experience as a unity, not as a succession of events. It is musical architecture on a noble scale, corresponding to the arias of opera and oratorio, in which soloist and orchestra alternate and interweave their patterns and distill the essence from a single mood. Such movements stand at the end of a great tradition rooted in vocal art.

An equally ancient tradition persisted in the dance movements assembled in suites. Here the basic form was binary, the simplest of all patterns of thought or of activity: statement and response, outward journey and return. Melodic figures based on stylized dance rhythms gave thematic consistency, and modulation to a central cadence in the complementary key (the dominant or relative) provided formal shape. The symmetry of central and final cadences is the essential feature, whether in folk-dance or stylized Baroque suite. It was ensured by thematic identity at those corresponding points, even in textures like Bach's which are otherwise fluid and contrapuntal. More still, the "galant" composers chose those two points at which to make their most ceremonious bows. The formalities of their approach to the first were matched in their withdrawal at the second. Suites of such pieces, along with opera overtures, served for the "table-music" and chamber-concerts of courts. It was in this music that players and composers found outlet for their talents, and an obvious opportunity to apply their instrumental technique to achieving more than Rococo bows at the cadences. They extended these closing sections, giving them the status of a separate theme, and an individual character which set them in contrast with the opening subject-matter. This reconciliation of opposites within a single movement was a new conception in music; it provided the basis of the new sonata form. It is possible to interpret these contrasts, which are purely musical in origin, as symbols of psychological differences, of the male and female principle, of heroism, tenderness, or grief; and to see in their musical working out a drama of human significance. The influence of association is so strong—and music had had a hundred and fifty years of it in connexion with opera—that such extra-musical comparisons can scarcely be avoided. But it is reasonable to assume these associations to be unconscious, and to see in the sonata form which was emerging a flexible means of achieving purely musical structure. That is how it came into being, and if in subsequent history it was turned to emotionally descriptive use, it does not follow that that is its only function. It is an expression of "mind" in music in the all-embracing sense of the word.

Because of its flexibility, sonata form* was able to provide a medium of musical communication for men of widely different

* To avoid ambiguity, the term sonata form is used here to apply to the structure of a single movement, consisting of an exposition of contrasted themes, their development, and their recapitulation. The general term sonata refers to a whole work which contains one or more movements organized in sonata form. Such a work for orchestra is called a symphony, and if for more than two players, a trio, quartet, etc.

mind. Haydn, Mozart, Beethoven, and Schubert showed its infinite range within the period loosely labelled "Classical", and their successors up to the present have found it an unfailing challenge to their musical and their expressive powers. It reached this central position because it brought about a new attitude to the development of musical material, a dynamic instead of a static view. The ritornello quoted in Ex. 6 shows a great curve of melody growing from germinal motives and forming an entity in itself. It is as stable, in its entirety, as a mountain peak whose slabs, shoulders, and pinnacles merge into a static mass. As the concerto proceeds, the curves of the ritornello sweep up at salient points as the outlines of single peaks repeat themselves in a mountain range. Between them there is contrast and relative repose, but in the total view they constitute a single and unmoving whole. That is the Baroque view of thematic development. When Haydn began his work, sonata movements had acquired one of their new defining features, the use of themes contrasting both in key and character. These were set against a background of traditional figural development, and this in itself need not involve a great departure from the static conception of a symmetrical movement, with themes A and B presented in an opening exposition, and returning at the end, after due discussion, in a balancing recapitulation. But dramatic possibilities were latent in the changing of key between subjects A and B, and in the preparation for recapitulation of A and B in the home key. If emphasis is laid on these processes of movement from one tonal plane to another; if the characteristics of one theme are set in high relief or shown in changing aspects by intensive development of motives; if these are set sharply over against the distinctive personality of another theme—it is clear that the very sounds of music can be invested with the quality of drama. It is clear too that if these themes carry suggestions of emotional import, sonata form can provide a powerful means of expression, significant in human as well as musical terms. It did in fact establish itself as the normal medium for serious musical thought, persisting through all subsequent changes of style, and holding a central place in the affections of music-lovers in general. There is little doubt that this is because of its adaptability to all moods, presenting them not in a static and stylized manner, but with a "truth to nature" which the ordinary person finds more congenial than "art for art's sake".

It is none the less true that the sonata was a purely musical growth; every stage of its expansion can be described exclusively in technical terms. It owed nothing to external stimulus of a literary or poetic kind. The 18th century was singularly devoid of this kind of inspiration until the 1770's, when the new musical forms were already fully defined. The sonata as a whole group of movements grew out of the Italian opera overture, with its three movements, quick-slow-quick. It absorbed the minuet from the suite (for instance in a symphony by the Viennese composer, Monn, in 1740, and Sammartini even earlier had used a four-movement plan). Innovations and adaptations were natural when all kinds of existing instrumental music were being called into service for concerts both public and private. No individual, no particular "school" of composers among those which were active in Italy, in Vienna, Mannheim, and Berlin, did more than contribute to a general development which arose from the nature of music itself. When it is freed from the specific demands of words, music must develop its own thematic material. The growth from binary form into the fully mature sonata form is a process of expansion in melodic range, in rhythmic variety, in harmonic and orchestral colour; an enrichment of subject-matter both in musical calibre and in the enlargement of the second subject into a composite group of themes; a widened scope of modulation, enhancing the drama of the return to the original key; a steady reabsorption of contrapuntal resource which heightens the intellectual interest and furthers the processes of development; an increasing awareness of the function of the coda in concluding an argument or confirming a mood. Only by listening and by study of musical scores can we turn these technical processes into living experience, but it is through them that music conveys the composer's conception to our minds. Its language reveals ever-new subtleties, and the experience it communicates is not attainable without an understanding of its forms. Poetry and drama, architecture and painting have their inner secrets, and do not disclose them to the casual observer. More elusive still is the real essence of musical thought (apart from the mere emotional effect of its sensuous sounds). It is not a representative art; it is not "about something", but is significant in itself. The achievement of the mid-18th century composers was to create the most flexible of forms in which musical thought can be expressed in terms of instrumental sound. Using this medium, without submission to hardened convention but with fresh creative imagination as each work unfolded its individual drama, Haydn, Mozart, Beethoven, and Schubert brought European music to a summit from which only descent was possible.

It is only possible here to refer to the general relation of these composers to their age. They are immortal through their genius, but Haydn and Mozart belonged entirely to the life and culture of the 18th century. They accepted its institutions, its musical language and forms. Although Haydn was steeped in the folk-music of the country, and retained his simple sturdy humanity, it would be a gross exaggeration to see in this a democratic influence in music. It gave breadth and geniality to his melody, sustained him in sincerity of feeling, and fed his ever-ready humour. But these qualities emerged in the ordinary pursuit of his calling, which was, first and last, to provide entertainment for courts and aristocratic audiences. That he could do this on such a high artistic level is due to the enlightened appreciation of patrons who had taste and education enough in music to recognize his genius and follow him step by step as he expanded the scope of his art. He had no cause to be a rebel. With Mozart, we are conscious simply of music, not of an age. We can imagine him in any period, transmuting the experiences of life into a pure art of sound. But in the brief span of his own life from 1756 to 1791, he drew together all the threads of contemporary music, and, moreover, he submitted his mind to the discipline and inspiration of J. S. Bach on the highest levels of musical thought. Out of these resources, Mozart fashioned a language which is comprehensible to the unlearned yet infinitely subtle in nuance. He used it with an artistry which is unsurpassed and which has remained an ideal for the most diverse of succeeding composers. He did this not only in what we now consider to be the purest realm of the art, in chamber-music and in his last great symphonies—a whole range of works in which he penetrated to regions of the spirit which only music can reach—but in every practical field which served the needs of life, in music for the church, for the theatre, or for incidental entertainment. In him, art and life are one. He had a supreme musical endowment, and at the same time an extraordinary power of human perception and feeling. It is possible to find some of his attributes in different men; none has his universal range, none attains his assured and unselfconscious art.

But is it only for his personal genius that Mozart holds a unique place in music? His name and Haydn's can be coupled

20. Vierzehn-Heiligen. Details of the roof at the crossing.

21. The New Opera House, Sydney, Australia. (Model.)

together, and though Mozart's is so much the finer spirit, soaring far beyond the age which for the most part kept Haydn for its own, they were entirely alike in using that age's forms of expression. They differed in the quality of their minds, but however different their personalities they shared the same language, with one another, and with the society to which they belonged. In that last great era of civilization music was fused with life. No doubt it brought richer reward to the persons educated to appreciate it, but there was nothing in its language that was foreign to the ordinary person, none of our present-day segregation of artistic and popular music. If we think onwards from that time to this, we shall not mistake evolution for progress.

SUMMARY

The undercurrents of thought and feeling which were preparing revolution against hardened absolutism in France did not disturb the calm exterior of society in 18th-century Germany and Austria. The German-speaking peoples had found a new spirit as passions calmed after their Reformation crisis. Their newly liberated genius found its first outlet in the stream of Protestant music which culminated in Bach, and in the glories of Baroque architecture stimulated by the Counter-Reformation. On the one hand was a bourgeoisie assimilating the latest ideas in science and art, enthusiastic for singing, and, in Austria especially, rich in talented players. On the other hand was an aristocracy, serene in its assumption of power and glory, dispensing that patronage on which artists had never ceased to depend, but which was so soon to disappear under the onslaughts of revolution. This society was enjoying its last half-century of calmly ordered life, belief, and thought, and in this environment, instrumental music dedicated to the pure pleasure of sound developed into an art of highest expressive significance. In this last quarter-century, too, the greatest works of German literature began to appear, and the philosophic works of Kant. Apart from a certain emotional stimulus which Haydn experienced in the early 1770's, literature bore little fruit in the work of contemporary composers. Music was perfecting its own language and forms. For the first time it became primarily an instrumental art, all verbal forms being secondary to music which was expressive and significant in its own terms, and subservient to no exterior thought. Indeed, Mozart showed how it could impose its forms on the operatic stage, not in stylized abstractions but with freedom to use its own unrivalled power to draw the essence from situation and character. In this, as in the pure instrumental art based on the sonata, music at this classic moment represented the highest expression of the European mind.

14

The Age of Goethe and Beethoven

BEETHOVEN (1770–1827) inherited the musical language and forms of Haydn, Mozart, and their prolific contemporaries. Although he brought a new power and a new emotional charge into music, the sonata remained for him, as it was for them, the normal medium of expression. Like his predecessors too, Beethoven was first and foremost a pure musician. This in spite of the fact that for a large number of people he speaks more eloquently than any other composer in directly human terms, conveying the emotion of moods of every kind. He did this with an intensity of personal feeling which was unprecedented in instrumental music, but he did not depend, for the direction of his thought, on the external stimulus of literary or pictorial images. In his single-minded pursuit of his own art he remained a classical composer, and so, in essentials, did his younger contemporary Schubert (1797–1828). They showed no departure from the traditional attitude of the professional musician, making music simply through inner compulsion, and unconsciously revealing their character in the process. But a new note nevertheless is unmistakable in their work. In addition to the expression of personal character (which indeed had been evident enough in the work of Haydn and Mozart), a new attitude to art becomes apparent, and a new relationship with society. This was induced by influences which had long been taking shape but which had not yet made an impact on that earlier generation.

The ideal of liberty was foremost among these influences, a natural tendency to react against hardened institutions both in life and thought. The storming of the Bastille by the Paris mob in 1789, and the collapse of clerical and aristocratic privileges in France, seemed to all Europe to promise a new age of freedom. How elusive that ideal was to be soon became apparent. The first results of revolution were a barbarous reign of terror and expansionist military ambition, provoking rigid conservative reaction throughout Europe after 1815, and a further half-century of alternation between monarchic and democratic pretensions. There was to be no short cut to a state of social equilibrium. But as far as political institutions can contribute to liberty, a stage of development was reached before the close of the 19th century, when parliamentary government had become established in all of Europe outside Russia. If human fellow-feeling demands at least a sharing of the basic necessities of life, we are bound to consider this stage to be an advance in social organization from one in which the populace went hungry for bread. But the mere attainment of parliamentary government is not the end of the quest for liberty. During the last two hundred years the problem has been restated in various ways, in terms of Nationalism, Socialism, Individualism, and a proliferation of -isms in the present century; for its solution we can only rely on the power of human genius to adapt itself to the challenges of life. On this note we can turn from the political to the literary search for freedom as it appeared in the 18th century.

The formalism of the French style, with its pseudo-Classical discipline, dominated much of the artistic life of Europe. England provided a healthy exception with a broadly-based literature, which ranged from the urbanity of Pope's polished couplets to the visions of Blake and his moments of high poetic beauty. The writings of Addison, Swift, Johnson, Gibbon, Hume, Goldsmith, and Sheridan are among the greatest treasures of our language. Each name recalls a fresh activity of mind, and in the newly emerging prose novel, Richardson, Fielding, and Sterne were developing still another medium for the study of human motives and conduct. Character and manners were the subject of drama in other parts of Europe. Molière's example had given the stimulus, and it bore fruit both in a new Danish literature, with the plays of Holberg (1684–1754), and in a refreshing of the older traditions of Spain, where Moratín (1760–1828) achieved both comedy and psychological insight which place him high among the century's dramatists. In Italy, Metastasio (1698–1782) was the central figure, both through his own literary and dramatic skill and through the predominance of opera, to which he contributed so many libretti. Along with him stand Gozzi and Goldoni, who lifted the old farce to the level of true comedy. The former, with a love of fantasy and fairy-tale combined with irony, remains in our contemporary memory as the author of *The Loves of the Three Oranges* and *Turandot*.

But the new creative force which broke through the crust of tradition was found in Germany, still not a nation, but a loose assembly of separate states united only by a subtle sense of ancient kinship. The German-speaking peoples had already shown in architecture and music the extent of their revitalization; in the mid-century they were on the eve of their greatest period of literature. Since the Thirty Years' War, the French style had appeared to present the only worthy model in literary as well as social convention, a situation that could not permanently satisfy the native genius. This external authority lay heavily on Gottsched, Professor of Poetry at Leipzig, who worked during the second quarter of the century to bring some unity into the German language itself and to raise the level of the theatre above vulgar farce and fantastic tragedy. While improving taste, he looked no further than the French dramatists for guidance. But his efforts to be a German Boileau provoked a controversy from which fruitful ideas emerged. Two Swiss professors, Bodmer and Breitinger, pleaded for imagination rather than regularity of form, and in pointing to Milton as an example, they turned the German mind towards English sources which henceforward proved to be singularly liberating and inspiring. Enthusiasm for Milton was one of the sources of inspiration for Klopstock (1724–1803). As the first of the new German poets he claims more attention than his intrinsic qualities would warrant, at any rate for the modern reader. In his grandiose epic *Der Messias*, whose twenty cantos appeared at intervals from 1748 to 1773, he used a new metre, the hexameter, and in his *Odes* exalting the ancient Germanic tradition he showed a rough vigour in varied rhymeless forms. If only in this metrical freedom, he broke the monopoly of the French Alexandrine, and gave a suggestion of the flexibility which Goethe was to consummate in his lyrics. Already we can see in Klopstock three of the influences which were to form the new literature: example and stimulus from England, consciousness of German national character, and a spirit of rebellion against the constraints of convention. England's influence was especially helpful in this latter respect. Her dramatists had shown that a play can have coherence as a living organism without depending on prescribed formulas, and they, and the contemporary novelists, showed how limitless is the scope for observation outside the elevated circles of heroic and mythological personages. Wieland (1733–1813) brought Shakespeare within reach by his translations, and his interest in the English novelists led to his *Agathon*, the first of a distinctively German genre, the psychological and pedagogic novel.

More powerful both in mind and influence was Lessing (1729–81), in whose critical writings and plays aspiration became solid achievement. Shakespeare held the foremost place in his thought about drama, exemplifying Aristotle's dictum that tragedy should "purge the emotions through pity and fear", not, as with Corneille, through the severity of its moral lessons. Lessing's own plays of middle-class life seem closer to the modern world, in theme and social atmosphere, than to the courts where at that very time music was adopting its classical form. The value Lessing set on folk-song recalls the gulf which was felt to exist between the conventions of aristocratic society and the truth of simple nature. But although he applied his art to the illumination of ordinary life, Lessing did more than anyone else to make clear the artist's function. In all his work as a journalist and critic he sought to clarify the thought of his generation. He gave a consciousness of the artist's function in society which was to be a distinctive feature of the new phase of mental activity, appearing first in German literature, and then in art generally with the 19th century.

The sense of the dignity of the artist, even of the superiority of his vision, is strongly present in Beethoven; it is one of the traits which separate him from his musical predecessors. In a letter from Bettina von Arnim to Goethe, these are some of the statements imputed to him: "Music is a higher revelation than all wisdom and philosophy", "Music, verily, is the mediation between intellectual and sensuous life", "Music is the one incorporeal entrance into the higher world of knowledge which comprehends mankind but which mankind cannot comprehend." Confident assertions of this kind show how the artist's relation to society was changing. Lessing provided much of the intellectual basis of this attitude; Herder gave it emotional impetus.

Herder (1744–1803) is notable not for any permanent value in his own writing, but for his influence, especially on Goethe. Like Rousseau, he looked to nature for inspiration which the Enlightenment failed to give to ardent souls. But in place of abstract notions concerning the blissful state of uncivilized man, he substituted an evolutionary view, that every age achieves artistic expression suited to its character, and that each reveals some fresh aspect of truth. The poet, in every age, was a heaven-sent genius, and he who would be a poet now must seek his inspiration in communion with the highest minds of the past. In this belief, Herder praised the creative genius of Homer and Shakespeare; he collected ballads and folk-songs of all nations, published in 1778–9 as *Stimmen der Völker in Liedern*; and he succumbed to the glamour of the Middle Ages. A group of lyrical poets, Claudius, Hölty, Bürger, responded to this stimulus in verse which received many musical settings in the following century. But more startling was an outburst of drama in a phase called *Sturm under Drang* (from the title of a play by von Klinger). The main figures of this episode of storm and stress—the angry young men of the 1770's—gave a liberal interpretation to Herder's protest against narrow convention. They were the opponents of all convention, social, moral, political, or literary. Nothing less than Shakespearian grandeur and passion would serve to conquer a new age in which the world should belong to the strong in will. The world has forgotten those ardent spirits, Lenz, von Klinger, Schubart, Leisewitz, and Müller, but it remembers one whose genius was fired during this glow of aspiration.

The mind of Johann Wolfgang Goethe (1749–1832) was all-embracing; he gathered up all the diverse strands of thought and literary expression of his age. In his universality, in his insight into human character, in his use of every medium of expression, from those which embrace the whole human scene to the lyrics of passionate individual experience, he is of the stature of the greatest of any age. But his copious writings do not form a homogeneous whole; they do not come to a focus in the same way as those of Dante, Cervantes, or Shakespeare, who seemed to bring to a white-hot centre the spirit of their respective ages. Goethe reflected the mind of his time, or rather he raised its thought to a far higher power, but the strands which ran through the 18th century were so sharply defined that they could not blend into a unity. This was inevitable, for at the time when the new German literature was coming into being, there seemed to be no new way of creation which did not involve at the same time criticism and destruction. And when assertion was made, it was in the name of individuals, not of a corporate mind. The dichotomy which existed in France, the apparently irreconcilable claims of reason and the heart, reappeared at every point in the literature of Germany. It revealed itself in Apollonian natures on the one hand—in Lessing and Winckelmann, with their

strong Classical predilections; and Dionysiac ones on the other—
in Herder and the dramatists of *Sturm und Drang*.

In the astonishing mind of Goethe, both attitudes are to be
found. He grew up in the rationalist tradition of Leipzig, and
he was always a fervent admirer of Greek civilization. But his
creative powers were liberated when Herder fired him with
enthusiasm for the directly human qualities in art. He experienced his own *Sturm und Drang*, a phase in which he
explored the theme of personal individuality: first, in its assertive
aspect, with *Götz von Berlichingen* (1773), a play which set
rebellious genius against the institutions of society; next, in its
passive aspect, with an analysis of morbidity in the novel
Werther (1774), which anticipated one of the moods of the
Romantics. More directly personal were the supreme lyrics which
sprang from his own passionate experiences, and in the same
glow of feeling and imagination he was working at *Faust* and
completed the scenes of Gretchen's betrayal. The Italian visit of
1786–8, however, contributed the sense of proportion so essential
to his insatiable nature, but far more important was its contribution to the harmony of his mind, to the balance of intellect and
emotion which characterized the work of his maturity.

Goethe's is one of the greatest minds of Europe, and one of
the most unusual. Supreme artist as he was in parts of his work,
we do not think of him exclusively as poet, dramatist, or novelist,
absorbed in art alone and unconsciously communicating the
spirit of an age. In this, he differs from Beethoven and Schubert,
the two great contemporaries of his later years; and from Schiller
too (1759–1805), essentially a dramatist and poet. We think of
Goethe as "the sage of Weimar", probing the mysteries and the
unsolved problems of life. His conversations and letters, fortunately so fully recorded, are an essential part of his mind. In his
inquiring attitude, his concern with man's place in the universe
in social and physical as well as spiritual matters, he is of the
modern world; but he transcends the purely scientific and the
purely philosophical approach through the power of his poetic
imagination. He had little respect for metaphysics, as appears in
Mephistopheles' ironic comments to the Student in *Faust*, or in
Eckermann's report of a conversation with Hegel: "I am certain
that many a dialectic disease would find a wholesome remedy in
the study of nature." With Goethe we stand at the cross-roads.
He is in the succession of men of the highest genius who speak
the language of art, but in thought he belongs to an age which

can accept neither religious dogma nor Renaissance assertion of individuality as ultimate certainties.

Attempts to capture truth in a net of logic were resumed in a series of formidable philosophical systems which began with Kant's *Critique of Pure Reason* (1781), and his *Metaphysic of Morals* (1785). To explain how the human mind can comprehend the material world, Kant assumes the existence of "things in themselves", and also the presence of faculties in our mind by which we can synthesize the materials presented to our senses. These faculties—"forms of intuition" about space and time, "categories of thought" about attributes and qualities, cause and effect—are implanted in our minds; they are transcendental, not derived from experience. Our knowledge can only be of the appearance of things as interpreted by these presumably God-given faculties. A new note which Kant introduced into his moral philosophy is interesting through its relation to the broader mind of the age. Again, this involves assumptions, of God's existence, of man's free-will, and of immortality. Man, for his part, is subject to the "categorical affirmative", a conception of moral duty as a law of nature. A rational being conforms to such law by his will, not for self-interest. He has the consolation of knowing that although virtue does not necessarily bring happiness on earth, God correlates virtue with happiness, and the hereafter exists so that man can reap his eventual reward. . . .

Kant's system can be left to the mercies of his brother philosophers. His theory of knowledge was soon abandoned. But the tone of his moral philosophy, with its call for the harmonization of man's will with an ideal moral law, is in keeping with the new temper of mind which we have seen already in Goethe, and which we associate especially with Beethoven. We must guard, as always, against the assumption that a composer sets out in an instrumental work to express any particular mood or thought. Beethoven, however, gives us strong clues to his general sympathies when choosing and setting words: in the theme of liberty and heroism in *Fidelio*, in the title *Eroica* for his Third Symphony, and in the setting of Schiller's *Ode to Joy* in the Choral Symphony. And apart from his music, his own views on the great issues of life are known: he believed in no personal God, but he was convinced of the reality of a spiritual power immanent in nature, and he had a sense of mission to communicate the uplifting power of his belief through his art. It is obviously absurd to suppose that such thought can be translated literally into musical sound; but it is not absurd to suggest that the states of mind and the emotions which the composer himself experienced should emerge unconsciously in his phraseology, his rhythms, his buildings of climaxes, and his alternation of tension and repose. By the time Beethoven began to compose, instrumental music had become a language so rich in associations that a composer who had command of its resources was using a medium in which he could scarcely avoid self-revelation. If he was a Dussek, he uttered platitudes; if a Beethoven, the quality and the orientation of his mind were inevitably apparent in his music.

Beethoven appeared at a time when all conditions were favourable to his genius and temperament. Serious by nature, and strengthened in character by early responsibilities, he grew to maturity in the noblest phase of German literature and moral philosophic thought. Assertively individual, he lived at a time when the ideal of liberty inspired both thought and action. Urgent in feeling and powerful in mind, he inherited a musical language which was already highly expressive, but capable of flexible expansion to meet his urgent demands. Unlike the poets and dramatists who had had to free themselves from an alien convention, Beethoven found in the sonata a living organism, not a stereotyped form. As a medium for conveying thought and feeling it is a musical counterpart to the drama, but not being restricted to direct representation and the physical limitations of the stage, it allows the composer to range over the whole realm of the spirit. The sonata has its own principles of artistic organization, and can communicate the highest aesthetic satisfaction through the endless scope it gives for securing formal order in sound. One part of Beethoven's greatness lies in his unsurpassed command of it as a purely artistic medium. The other lies in his assumption of the liberty to use it in expressing every human feeling. It is natural to crave for liberty, though so often the ideal remains an abstraction. But at some moments in history, the conception has become a reality, in strange and unexpected ways. Ancient Athens found expression of her genius when freed from the Persian menace; ordinary humanity was given spiritual release from formal religion by Jesus of Nazareth; Giotto freed the art of painting from subservience to external abstractions; Monteverdi set music on a new road by breaking with a convention which was not appropriate for his expressive purposes. Beethoven in his turn brought a new freedom, not by discarding an artistic convention, but by bringing within its scope a new range of human experiences. Michelangelo offers the closest parallel in art, employing Renaissance forms, but displaying a titanic energy which made new developments imperative to successors who did not possess his reserves of power. Beethoven had the same masterful energy; none fought more heroic battles of the spirit than he. They were his own personal struggles, of deeply individual import even in his setting of the Mass. They might, as in the Third and Fifth Symphonies, show man seeking reconciliation with the external forces of the world; or they might represent, as in the last string quartets, the search for peace within his own soul. Besides these strenuous moods, all those others are to be found that spring from a generous nature, and from the positive spirit of a man who, though afflicted by deafness during most of his working life, turned a courageous face to the world.

SUMMARY

German literature in the second half of the 18th century records the successive stages, in criticism, constructive thought, and imaginative creation, by which Europe passed from the acceptance of absolutism to assertion of individualism in things of the mind. All aspects of this process of transition are visible in Goethe, through whose breadth and sanity as well as artistic genius the transformation took place with a tranquillity which contrasted with contemporary political stresses. In Beethoven the assertion of individualism was complete, but it was expressed in terms of a highly organized musical form which prevented a descent into mere subjectivism. Beethoven, in this respect, stood at the end of an era in which music still had universal significance, while at the same time he was the most powerful figure among many whose musical activities were beginning to show the pattern of a new individualistic age.

15

The Creative Mind: Individualism

ON 20th April 1791, Louis XVI and Marie Antoinette attended
a performance at the Académie for the last time. They saw
Rameau's *Castor et Pollux*, one of those serious operas which
could have been heard at any time during the previous century
and a half in any court or opera-house in Europe. Like the royal
régime, this aristocratic art was coming to its end, and with it an
age in which music had served a universal purpose in relation to
society. Portents of change had appeared even before the Revolution. The musical stage in France had adopted many new themes
in response to a widening bourgeois interest and sentiment, and
as this new public replaced the older patronage it made increasingly varied demands in art and entertainment. Authors
and composers too, for their part, had new views about their
function. We have seen something of their individualist assertion
in German literature, and in Beethoven's exalted conception of
the artist's mission. Literary and musical output consequently
began to reflect so many different social needs and varied creative
trends, that the European scene in the 19th century appears
crowded and confused if we try to see it as a whole at any one
moment. It is easier to find a true perspective if we follow the
separate trends of thought and art down to our own day. No
longer does any uniform attitude pervade society as a whole. On
the contrary, an ever-widening gulf appears between the public
and the artist, who now becomes engrossed in the private cultivation of his art. The purely artistic developments which arose
from this individualist approach are the subject of the present
chapter; social aspects of art and thought will be discussed in
the next.

I

Individualism had been a leading theme in the literature of
Sturm und Drang, with its ardent faith in genius and its admira-
tion of the high-minded rebel against society. This was a phase

of opposition to convention, and of emotional reaction against rationalism. It foreshadowed to some extent the Romanticism which took hold of Europe at the end of the century. But although Romanticism was primarily concerned with all that is remote from the matter-of-fact world of the here and now, it was not merely negative and escapist. It sprang from a conviction that man's highest experiences are to be found not in the purely physical and rational domain, but in harmony with an all-pervasive spirit which is immanent in nature. This attitude had affinity with the mysticism of Boehme and the pantheistic philosophy of Spinoza. It was given conscious formulation as a system of thought and aesthetics by the brothers Schlegel at the turn of the century, and it accounted for many of the apparently unrelated interests of the writers, painters, and musicians during the next fifty years.

For the Romantics, nature herself was a constant source of inspiration, in her wild and terrible as well as gentler moods. This interest included, but also extended far beyond, an appreciation of the beauties of scenery. Wordsworth (1770–1850), whose poetry was the fruit of meditation in our own Lakeland environment, did not indulge in extravagant moods, but he showed the direction of the new trend. Using words with their plain meanings he produced an emotional impact unweakened by artificialities of poetic diction, and in his reflections on simple experiences of life he opened a new vein of psychological suggestion and intuition. This straightforward attitude to nature appeared in much of the great lyric poetry of this age of personal effusion. The appeal of Goethe, Schiller, Heine, Eichendorff, Rückert, and Mörike, is obvious in the songs of Schubert, Schumann, Brahms, and Wolf; and Weber brought the very atmosphere of nature into German opera in Der Freischütz and Oberon. But the Romantic spirit explored further, more deeply, and above all, more through emotional experience than through reflection. Coleridge evoking mystery, Blake calling up visions from the unconscious, Shelley, Byron, Keats exploring new regions of poetic passion, visual image, and sensual delight; Rückert seeking spiritual inspiration from the East (a source of many new influences in the 19th century); E. T. A. Hoffmann creating a supernatural world of fiction with its own meanings underlying human experience; the magical and macabre lurking in the background for poets, painters, and musicians, as in Marschner's operas, Weber's music for the Haunted Glen scene in *Der Freischütz*, and Goethe's Walpurgis Night in *Faust*; all the legend, fear, and fantasy that has gathered about nature in the imagination of past and present were vivid in the poetic mind of the age.

Obsessed with the idea that contemporary society was decadent, some Romantic writers looked for a pristine purity in peoples who had not been subjected to the baleful influence of civilization. Rousseau had generalized about the "noble savage"; Chateaubriand (1768–1848) found his particular ideal in the American Indian. His writing was eloquent. That of Sir Walter Scott (1771–1832) was less naïve, in historical novels which captured the imagination of Europe by recalling the ideals and atmosphere of medieval chivalry and scenes of the living past. Victor Hugo (1802–85) brought verve and poetic vision to the pageantry of former times, and Pushkin (1799–1837)—the Goethe, and almost the creator of Russian literature—struck his roots deeply into native soil at a time when the Eastern and Western minds were making their first real contacts. His *Boris Godunov* lived again later in the music of Mussorgsky, and with it, the soul of the Russian people, as in so many of the great novels of the later century. A similar devotion to national tradition had fired the German literary pioneers of the 18th century, and this enthusiasm received fresh stimulus through the Romantic nostalgia for a nobler past. Tieck (1773–1853), one of the acknowledged leaders of the new movement, wrote his *Volksmärchen* (literary fairy-tales), the brothers Grimm produced their collection of traditional German folk-tales, and Arnim and Brentano collaborated in collecting and publishing folk-songs, under the title *Des Knaben Wunderhorn*, a work which strengthened Romantic awareness of the rich heritage of the past.

Endlessly introspective in seeking to harmonize their own minds with the universal spirit of nature, the poets and novelists had an ever-present sense of man's insufficiency. A prevailing note of melancholy ran through their thought, amounting to a preoccupation with the theme of death (Novalis), and to actual suicide and unbalance of mind in several cases. The mood was tense at times and full of despair (the plays of von Kleist), indignant and rebellious (Victor Hugo and Lermontov, Pushkin's contemporary in Russia), resentful of society's indifference to the artist, so necessary to its well-being (Alfred de Vigny, Borel), addicted to self-pity (Lamartine), full of wistful remembrance of childhood as the golden age of happiness (Alfred de Musset, and

Verlaine; in Mallarmé also, with his new poetic language in which symbols replaced sequential statement, and in Rimbaud, who thought to widen sensibility by a mingling of sensuous effects. Stefan George (1868–1933), and Rilke (1875–1926), carried aestheticism and symbolism into German poetry, and assumed with highest seriousness the rôle of poet-seers. Decadence and dandyism in a brilliant English circle of the 1890's, violence and depravity in D'Annunzio (1863–1938), were but extreme manifestations of the spirit of doubt among the men of letters in a bourgeois world of smug belief in progress.

II

Some Romantic visionaries had longed for a union of the arts, and aesthetes in the later century sought for musical sounds and cadences in their verse, and poetical impressions in their music. It is interesting to see how the painters and musicians themselves interpreted their own several functions. With the waning of private patronage, painters lost security of position but gained scope for individual expression. When thrown on their own resources they could give rein to imagination both in choice and in treatment of subject. This fact alone brought about an enlargement of artistic experience, first in a phase which involved no real break with tradition, and then, from the 1880's, in a new attitude which brought to an end the era which Giotto had initiated. A common factor underlying all the differences of personal method which ensued was the artist's increasing preoccupation with the problems of his art, as a painter, not as a servant of society. This became pronounced with the work of the Impressionists after the mid-century, and after that it overrode all considerations of public need or approval.

In the first phase painters were still concerned with representation of the world as they saw it, but with ever more individual vision. The serenely ordered landscapes of Poussin gave place to the more arresting detail of Constable (1776–1837), to the dazzling colour and poetic imagination of Turner (1775–1851), and the stranger moods and remoter scenes of nature in Friedrich (1774–1840) and his Romantic contemporaries. Already in the 18th century, Hogarth's social commentaries had reached a widening public even while Reynolds and Gainsborough were painting their fashionable portraits. Goya (1746–1828) probed mercilessly below pretentious exteriors at the Spanish court, and

Delacroix (1799–1863), rebelling in his turn against the heroic poses of the Revolution's official art, indulged his passion for colour and for capturing the exciting moment. The insular Pre-Raphaelite movement in England aimed also, in its own precious manner, to escape from the Renaissance tradition of consciously composed groupings. Beside these changing attitudes to scenes and personalities, new themes appeared, ranging from the inner visions and fantasies of Blake (1757–1827), and Goya too, to Millet's scenes of peasant life, and the unposed realism of Courbet (1819–77). And, in a final chapter of the story of natural representation, the appearance of painting was transformed by a new perception of physical factors involved in vision. Manet (1832–83), and the Impressionists who followed him (Monet, Sisley, Pissarro, and with different emphasis, Degas, Renoir, Whistler) administered shocks to contemporary taste, but this was more through their technical methods than through any fundamental change in their view of the artist's attitude to nature. They were concerned to record the image which impresses itself at the moment of vision, not the full detail of a scene which we complete with our minds. "Light is the most important personage in a picture", said Manet, and the study of its properties, both through the science of optics and through analysis of its effect on things seen, absorbed these enthusiasts for accurate visual impressions. Their work is familiar, with its "pointillisme", its absence of sharply outlined edges, and its coloured shadows and shimmering light. Far from being the hasty daubing of poetical dreamers, it constituted one more stage in the quest for truth as perceived by the eye. Sculptors too, like Rodin (1840–1917), concentrated attention on just those elements which were essential to their artistic conception; the rest of the stone could be left unworked.

From the time of the first "Salon des refusés" in 1863, when the advanced painters of the day held their own exhibitions and declared their independence of academic standards, the relationship between artist and public began to change. With no violent movement on the surface there occurred a quiet revolution. Whether the public at some time in the future might come to like what they were doing was beside the point for the artists: they had passionate convictions now. They were prepared to be rejected, but not to compromise on the principles of their art. The Impressionists had not "rebelled" against tradition; they were using new knowledge in presenting the world as they saw it. Neither were their immediate successors, Cézanne, Van Gogh, Gauguin, conscious of any real cleavage. They too based their art upon nature, but with a stress upon features which concerned them as artists, not as imitators. It was through their devotion to the ideals of art, with no reference to the ideals of society, that these Post-Impressionists brought an old era to a close, and laid the foundations of the one which has prevailed in the 20th century. Cézanne (1839–1906) was intent to bring out the forms which are inherent in nature itself, not to impose an arbitrary order of his own. The solid outlines of rocks, the slant of branches, the basic geometrical shapes of roofs or of hillsides should convey the sense of depth and the interrelation of forms. This, for Cézanne, was to penetrate to the essential character of a scene. Its solidarity and depth were more important to him than the detail of correct perspective, and so were the relationships of forms and colours in his studies of still life. From this concern for the simple forms to be found in nature it was a short step to a purely constructional interest in shapes and designs themselves. The illustrations by Aubrey Beardsley, the poster art of Toulouse Lautrec, the exquisite designs of Matisse, belong to this phase of decorative simplification. It remained for Braque and Picasso (born 1881) to explore the possibilities of imaginative creation with geometric forms alone—Cubism and the purely abstract compositions which have followed are the logical results of Cézanne's revolution.

Like Cézanne, Van Gogh (1853–90) could have formed no conception of the developments which would follow his short impassioned spell of painting in the few years before his death. He learnt the vivid use of colour from the Impressionists, but this, for him, was to be a positive means of self-expression, a communication of living sympathy and ardent exaltation. He painted as a lonely individual under the compulsion of his own excited feeling, with a personal out-giving which had not been characteristic of visual art. This potentiality for the release of the artist's own emotion, either of fellow-feeling with the sufferings and passions of humanity, or simply in terms of line and colour, gave a point of departure for the "Expressionists", notably Klee and Kandinsky working in Germany, and for such non-representational work as the current "action painting". Still another break with the tradition of idealizing nature as seen through purely European eyes was accentuated by Gauguin (1848–1903), seeking simplicity in the South Sea Islands, and

bringing the primitive attitude to bear with his stark outlines
and patches of strong colour. This quickening of feeling and
imagination from unsophisticated sources was a stimulus to
Picasso in his early days, and it had a close parallel in the
Surrealism and dream-imagery (Salvator Dali), which some found
to be their response to Freud's revelations about the unconscious
mind.

Sculpture followed the same trends as painting, from Rodin's
vivid impressions of fully living figures, through Epstein's reflections of various contemporary phases, to the creations of Henry
Moore (born 1898), which seem to emerge as suggestions from
the stone itself, and not as copies of nature. In this, they are
products of the artist's own mind and not of the desire of a
community for symbols of faith or of a corporate way of living.
The visual artist has retired into his private world, not at all
with the melancholy of the Romantic poets who withdrew from
a materialist and insensitive society, but simply with a desire to
explore the problems of a still developing art. Van Gogh made
the attitude clear when he said: "The public will see nothing
but caricature in this exaggeration, but what does that matter
to us?" Perhaps it does not matter if the public needs time to
catch up with new artistic vision; what does matter is that it
should have the opportunity.

III

Music in the 20th century has reached the same position as the
other arts: composers are looking inwards, absorbed by the endless possibilities of their medium. This is a reversal of the
previous century's practice, with its extraordinary development
of music's descriptive and suggestive powers, and it is especially
understandable in an art which can have independent existence
purely in terms of sound. But pure formal order did not interest
the Romantic age, and music lent itself above all arts to the
enhancement of emotion and to the heightening of expressive
effect. Most of the 19th century's music was charged with strong
personal feeling; many of its particular developments occurred
through its association with external ideas.

The first of these characteristics was highly developed both in
Beethoven and Schubert. In so far as it is an unconscious revelation of character, it is present in all men of genius, and is not an
exclusively romantic attribute. Schubert's music glows with its

own unique intensity, quite apart from the specific moods of his songs. It makes a personal communication. The pathos of the Unfinished Symphony, or the lonely meditative opening of the C major Symphony would have been quite out of place in the social world of the 18th century. In fact, these particular works found no audience at all until long after the composer's death. Beethoven, by his playing and his forceful personality, succeeded better in imposing himself on the musical life of Vienna, and gave uninhibited expression to individual moods and feelings, especially in his piano sonatas and sets of variations. (His last five introspective string quartets remained a closed book for his contemporaries.) Short pieces for the pianoforte, which was now becoming an increasingly flexible instrument, provided an appropriate medium for intimate expression. The small stream of instrumental lyricism, already apparent in Schubert, grew rapidly into a flood with the first piano works of Chopin (1810–49), Schumann (1810–56), and Liszt (1811–86), which began to appear in the 1830's. If the Romantic writers' ideal of a fusion of the arts was realizable at all, it was achieved by Chopin—though in a more purely musical sense than theirs— in his sublimation of pianoforte sound into pure poetry, and by Schumann, in his translation of mood and character into music. Separate pieces with no complications of form, or groups of independent pieces, appealed to Romantic composers for the expression of single moods, more than the sonata, with its ordered presentation of the contrasts of life. In some cases, even when the sonata was used, the revolt of the personal against the universal was evident, as in Liszt's attempt at a unified whole in his B minor Sonata, and in the concern for thematic unity shown by César Franck (1822–90). This appeared even more clearly in new attitudes to the symphony. The pianoforte continued and has never ceased to be an apt medium for self-revelation: for Mendelssohn's facile skill, for the virtuosity and descriptive imagery of Liszt; for the deep feeling of Brahms (1833–97) combined with a German seriousness of thought; for the French refinement of sentiment in Fauré (1845–1907), colourful impressionism in Debussy (1862–1918), and the finely drawn decorations of Ravel (1875–1937); for the piquant flavour of the lyricism of Grieg (1843–1907), and for the accomplishments of musicians of all countries in the present century, fed by their national cultures as well as by the main European tradition, such as

Rachmaninov, Bartók (1881–1945), and the British Bax, Ireland, and Frank Bridge.

In the *Lied*, or song in which the piano contributes equally with the voice to the musical interpretation of a poem, the 19th century found another of its most characteristic forms. German musicians especially were conscious of the glorious rebirth of their literature, which owed so much to the stimulus of an ancient heritage of song, and in its turn produced such a harvest of lyrical beauty. Schubert grew up with song and melody around him in Vienna, and with Mozart's example before him in the interplay of voices and instruments. A similar unity of voice and piano marked Schubert's songs from the beginning, and remained thenceforward a defining feature of this intimate art of expression. Here too the personal traits of composers emerged: Schubert's unsurpassed gift of melody and his unique power to embody poetic thought in musical theme and texture; Schumann's warm pianistic style and literary sympathy through which he matched words with a perfect musical counterpart; Brahms, rich in musical resources and memory of German folksong, unwilling to sacrifice the moulding of his melody to the rhythmical demands of words; Hugo Wolf (1860–1903), on the other hand, meticulous in accentuation and elaborate in pictorial suggestion; Richard Strauss (1864–1949) carrying on the Romantic tradition with his own particular glitter of harmony and texture; Mahler (1860–1911), at his best when responding to the specific suggestion of words, producing what is virtually the orchestral *Lied*; and, as always, the musical genius of France succeeding in conveying passion with restraint in the dozen or so exquisite songs by Duparc, and in the strangely evocative "mélodies" of Fauré, with economy rare even for a Frenchman, but with astonishing warmth of feeling, and poetical beauty in the delicate filigree of his accompaniments. National as well as personal characteristics found outlet in the song, either through deliberate cultivation of folk tradition, as in Russia and countries which had not hitherto contributed to the main stream of composition, or revealing themselves unconsciously as in such different men as Parry, Stanford, and Britten, with typically British sensitivity to literature.

The individualism so characteristic of the 19th century impressed itself on large-scale works of the sonata type as well as calling into being the more intimate forms associated with the piano and with solo-song. In the symphony, in concerted chamber music, and in solo-sonatas for various instruments, the principle of the classical sonata form persisted, and with varying degrees of modification* it has kept its vitality up to the present day. The musical situation in the 19th century strongly resembled that of the visual arts after the High Renaissance. The post-Classical musicians showed the same enjoyment of warm colour and personal mannerism as did the Venetian painters and 17th-century architects in Rome, but in both cases the purely artistic forms of the preceding "classic" phase provided the framework within which personal feeling could find expression. Thus, the emotionally charged melody which Beethoven brought into music but always kept subsidiary to organic development of motives was made by his Romantic successors to carry increasing weight in the symphonic structure. The allurement of Schubert's melodies and magical modulations may compensate for repetitions and mere fillings-in—the unique Unfinished Symphony standing beyond all cavil—but his music already presaged a decline from the pure symphonic ideal. The obtrusion of personal feeling brought loss in poise and universality, but endless opportunity for imaginative creation in an age of assertive individuality. Schumann, in his symphonies and chamber music, achieved lyrical beauty and deeply felt moods attainable only in a large instrumental setting. Personalities as different as those of Mendelssohn, Borodin, Glazounov, Tchaikowsky, Saint-Saëns, Bizet, César Franck, Dvořák, Brahms, Elgar, Sibelius, Vaughan Williams, Walton, and Shostakovitch showed what rich variety of musical experience could be communicated through this most flexible medium. In music as in the other arts, the creative impulse found continuous renewal within the artistic convention developed through the stimulus of the Renaissance.

Classical forms could provide a medium for much of the purely musical thought of the 19th century, individualistic as it was; but the Romantic obsession with all that is remote from orderly civilized existence encouraged musicians to apply their art to many new descriptive purposes. If music had developed such an expressive language in association with human emotions, could it not extend its applications to include external scenes and images, and with the help of literary suggestion use the magic of

---

* Some experiments in using transformation of a single theme and cross-references between movements showed an inclination to impose a narrow and literal view of musical homogeneity on a form which already possesses unity through the spiritual affinity of all its parts.

sound to reveal new worlds of imagination? Had not Beethoven imitated the sounds and varied aspects of nature in his Pastoral Symphony, and created in his *Leonore* Overtures a musical analogue of the moods and situations of the whole opera? Weber's translation of the atmosphere of forest and fairyland into orchestral sound, and Mendelssohn's evocative music in concert overtures such as *Fingal's Cave* and *Midsummer Night's Dream* left no doubt about the suggestive power of music, in alliance with external scenes and concepts. Romanticism produced some of its most colourful and exciting manifestations in the works of a succession of composers who sought to make music a counterpart to the kaleidoscope of nature, history, romance, and the creations of poetic imagination. Weber, Schumann, Berlioz, Liszt, and Wagner all had strong literary leanings. It was through Shakespeare, Walter Scott, and Goethe that the imagination of Berlioz (1803–69) was stimulated, and it was through scenes and passions already transmuted into poetry that his own musical thought was so often precipitated. The calm beauty that he attained at times made less impression on his century than the impassioned feeling, the vivid effect of orchestral colour and mass, which he brought to the enhancement of non-musical conceptions. The intensity of his conviction about the "expressive" function of music placed him in the avant-garde of musical Romanticism, and, more practically, his use of the *idée fixe*, or recurring motto-theme, appealed to his contemporaries as a telling device for narrative and programmatic purposes. More striking still was the contribution of Liszt to the pictorial apparatus of music. Given an informative title or an appended programme of words, a piece of music might be made to correspond to moods or scenes thereby suggested. The *idée fixe* which Berlioz had used as a thread might be subjected to transformation in rhythm or in harmony, and so suggest a continuity of existence through changing experiences. Liszt invented the term "Symphonic Poem", an apt description of a musical genre designed to reflect an external programme. His orchestral and pianistic works started a vogue. They suggested an appropriate outlet for composers who found classical forms restrictive of poetic fancy, and for those, like the Russians, Finns, and Czechs who had no symphonic tradition but a wealth of legend and story which could come to new life through this expressive musical medium. The symphonic poem was one of the characteristic creations of the 19th-century mind, revealing its essential individualism in composers as different as Franck and Debussy, Delius and Elgar, Sibelius and Strauss. The last-named carried it to extremes of realist and psychological suggestion, enhanced by musical and orchestral virtuosity.

Unique even in this century of assertive personality was the genius of Richard Wagner (1813–83), whose work represented a supreme union of music with the extra-musical. Its avowed aim was to achieve a fusion of music, drama, and spectacle, in a closer integration than that of traditional opera, from which it stood apart in a world of its own. It only came to fruition, in fact, under exceptional conditions of patronage by King Ludwig II of Bavaria, in the theatre opened at Bayreuth in 1876, a singular instance of a purely individual conception of art impressing itself on national character. For in pursuing his theories, which envisaged a musico-poetic language of universal significance transcending the narrowly personal, Wagner used the shadowy figures of Germanic legend and myth, and evoked in his music the scenes and the spirit of forest and mountain, and of the Rhine, which was the very symbol of German nationhood. He gave to his compatriots the musical conception of their fatherland, glimpsed partially by Weber before him, an artistic revelation similar to that which poets since Chaucer had given to England. This musical panorama alone revealed a new and wonderful aspect of the Northern mind. It was expressed with a sensuous beauty of melody and harmony and an exhilaration of feeling which ensured a lasting popular appeal. But beyond these obvious attractions, Wagner's music-dramas opened astonishing ranges of musical thought. Their fascination lies in the use of a musical language of *Leit-motive* (leading-motives or symbols), associated with every element, physical or psychological, in the drama. The characters themselves are by no means drawn from life; they are little more than personifications of the attributes of humanity, or agents of the forces of destiny. But the richly suggestive musical symbolism, introduced step by step with each visual and conceptual situation in the drama, gives the listener a key to every thought which is presented, for the most part in a flow of orchestral sound of symphonic dimension and development. We may not be convinced by Wagner's cosmology in *Der Ring*, or interested in his pseudo-philosophy, even if we warm to his romantic picture of the Mastersingers; but we can find neverending cause for wonder at the nuances of his self-created language, the fertile imagination by which he conceived and maintained a totally distinct idiom for *Der Ring*, for *Tristan und Isolde*, for *Die Meistersinger*, and the magnificence of his music, which although dedicated to extraneous ideas, emerges triumphantly after all as sheer music.

There is little wonder that this "music of the future" was intoxicating to many people. Its influence was felt in general ways, for instance by the literary Symbolists in France, as well as by particular musicians such as Franck, d'Indy, Wolf, Strauss, Humperdinck, and others who made use of its descriptive methods. The symphony itself was diverted to non-musical ends, in Bruckner's vast tracts of earnest mysticism, and as a last flicker of Romanticism in Mahler's mixture of morbid self-analysis and grandiose world-visions, built upon strangely insignificant musical materials with consummate orchestral skill. But more universal than such local instances was the effect of Wagner's enrichment of the whole harmonic and orchestral language of music. His chromaticism (and Liszt's), and the mordant orchestral polyphony of Strauss, brought music to a point where fresh thinking was inevitable. Schönberg (1874–1951) chose to adopt all semitones on an equal footing regardless of their function in relation to a tonic. He adopted the attitude of the German Expressionist painters (with whom he was at one time associated) and developed a technique in which complex structure had its fascinations and might yield artistic inspiration. Much experiment has followed these lines since the 1920's, and the present search for musical order produced by electronic means is another stage on this journey. Debussy gave the initial impetus to another reassessment of musical materials. Sound-groups chosen for their sensuous effect might form the basis of a language which need have little reference, or none, to the traditional grammar and syntax of music. Comparison with Impressionist painting is obvious, and subsequent developments led, as with the painters, to a preoccupation with the ordering of sounds for their own significant interest. Bartók and Stravinsky (born 1882) have pursued this line of experiment, the latter sharing Picasso's open-minded curiosity and readiness to embark on ever-new courses.

SUMMARY

Our rapid flight across the last century and a half has done scant justice to the work and personality of many men of genius. It has only permitted a sketch of some of the aspirations and achievements, the disillusions and renewed efforts of members of a European community of nations no longer sustained by a common ideal, religious, social, or artistic. The 19th century began with high hopes for the destiny of peoples and individuals emerging from restricting conventions. It ended with many notes of doubt among artists unsure of their place in an increasingly industrial age, and it has been followed by a half-century of reorientation within private worlds of art. It remains for us to see what tendencies may be at work towards a reintegration of the European mind.

16

The Creative Mind and Society

I

SOCIAL changes which followed the Revolution of 1789 affected not only the style and character of art, but also standards of taste. As art developed in the European courts and contributed continuously to the graces of life, the taste of its sponsors was inevitably formed by the beauties which surrounded them, and in the case of the musical aristocracy of Austria it was fortified by active participation and understanding. The disappearance of that joint tradition of creation and appreciation deprived the artist of more than his security; it left him dependent on the support of a public which had its own views on art. If these were not compatible with the artist's own convictions, what was he to do? He could go his own way and risk survival and success. In the last chapter we saw some of the achievements of this uncompromising individualism. They were not gained without cost: Berlioz financing his own concerts to obtain a hearing for his music, Wagner failing, but for the support of an eccentric king, to gain a foothold in the theatre; disillusion, sometimes suicide, but always the compulsion to create. On the other hand, public tastes were insistent too, and the mind of modern Europe has revealed itself in the kinds of demand made upon art and the place accorded to it in life.

An early example of box-office trends is seen in the fate of the Augarten concerts in Vienna. They were held in the garden which the Emperor Joseph II had dedicated to public use, and from 1782 their programmes regularly included great works by Mozart and Beethoven. But standards declined under successive managements; music of this calibre was not "popular" in appeal, but rather the dance-music of Pamer, Lanner, and Johann Strauss. (When we remember the charm of these *Ländler* and *Waltze*, we can only think ruefully of the state to which unscrupulous commercialism has reduced our present-day popular entertainment.) But even in concerts which made serious pretensions, programmes and standards reflected the unformed taste of a miscellaneous public who were assuming the patronage of music. All accounts of conditions in Europe in the first half of the 19th century agree in painting a picture of entertainments of little musical value in which chief store was set on the performances of singers or exhibitions of instrumental soloists. The chasm which existed between this new public and the truly creative mind was poignantly revealed in the respective careers of Robert and Clara Schumann, the composer exploring the inner world of his imagination, while his devoted wife toured the cities of Europe employing her fine pianistic talents in tawdry displays which provided their chief means of subsistence. The situation was scarcely new as far as the public was concerned; they have demanded entertainment from the days of mime and minstrel to those of television.

But this new public was now throwing up its own rulers and leading figures, and as the 19th century progressed it was also developing the institutions through which artistic effort could at last be maintained. Vienna, once more, shows the pattern which was emerging. The Gesellschaft der Musikfreunder (founded in 1813 like the Royal Philharmonic Society in London) extended its activities with a Singing Society in 1858 and an orchestral one in 1859. More significantly still, the Court Opera Orchestra, in giving its public performances from 1842, provided the Viennese with their first professional concerts. In Europe generally by the mid-century, properly rehearsed concerts were superseding the "run-through" held together by the principal violinist, and orchestras organized for concert purposes were replacing those drawn casually from the operatic theatre. With the development of these concert institutions and their subscribing public, the conversion of Court- into State-Opera houses (except in England, where private management since 1732 has contrived to keep Covent Garden as a venue for international opera); with the constant technical improvement of instruments, the increasing vitality of Conservatoires for professional training in music, and the wide dissemination now provided by broadcasting and the gramophone, the European scene has acquired the features which are common to-day. Through these channels the main tradition of music is maintained which had its origin in the worship of the ancient Church, flourished in the Renaissance and 18th-century courts as an adjunct of civilized life, and is now within the reach of any who are interested to receive it. It is available through the efforts of the small minority of people who consider it of value. It is by no means a corporate expression of the 20th-century mind, or even one of the graces of life for the men of "progress", the Henry Fords for whom "history is bunk", or the countless thousands who flee from the boredom of compulsory education to passive addiction to their sport and entertainment.

For the music-loving minority, a situation has developed during the last century which never existed before: the greatest part of the concert repertoire is drawn from music of the past. Contemporary composers are busy—they always will be, since the creative urge can never be suppressed—but in this century it is not easy for listeners to make contact with the new music of the day. The basic language of music has changed as radically as that of the visual arts, and with it the composer's power to communicate with any but the sophisticated listener. It may be that a commonly understood language will emerge for the general music-lover, but there is no certainty that any particular form of contemporary music will make more than a partial contribution to that end. Young enthusiasts welcome all that is new, but there is little in the successive phases of 20th-century experiment which gives the general listener the sense of human experience in music which he has found in composers from Bach to Brahms. Creative minds at present are less interested in human communication than in problems of musical structure. This is one reason for the prominence of older music in our programmes. Another lies in our stronger sense of history and greater awareness of our cultural heritage. Romantic writers had found stimulus in the variety and vigour of the Middle Ages, as well as escape from a colourless present. But historical interest is also a part of the intellectual search which characterizes the modern mind and impels it to seek a foundation of fact for its beliefs. Both these attitudes appeared in the resuscitation of the music of Bach, and Palestrina, in revision of plainsong, and in biographies and research which have multiplied since the end of the age of Beethoven. A great deal of the musical activity which hitherto had gone directly to musical creation was diverted from that time to non-creative ends of research and performance—a very significant pointer to the passing of the age which began with the Renaissance and found its pre-eminent expression in art.

After the decline of 18th-century *opera seria*, music for the stage became a faithful mirror of national and social characteristics. In Italy, devoted as always to vocal melody, opera occupied the central position in musical life, and it still retains its pre-eminence. It provided a natural outlet for passionate feeling and impetuous action, especially chiming with the mid-19th century mood of a people longing for the political liberation and unity of their country. The operas of Verdi (1813–1901) embodied these national characteristics, but more still they showed the power of individual genius to influence the general mind. He began his career when the average opera in the public theatres of Italy was tricked out with the showy vocal ornamentations of tasteless singers. Gleams of real quality, as in the comedy of Paisiello and Cimarosa, the melodic charm of Bellini, and occasional works like Donizetti's *Don Pasquale*, or Rossini's *Barber of Seville*, were rare and exceptional. It was Verdi's achievement, while accepting the unquestioned primacy of the voice to turn it from trivial uses and make it serve genuine dramatic purposes. In the fifty-five years which separated his first and last works, he not only matured his own powers in orchestral and dramatic ensemble, but brought his public, always captivated by his melodic allure, to the position of appreciating works like *Otello* and *Falstaff*, in which he brought a glow of Italian imagination to the great conceptions of Shakespeare.

Italian operas and performers were ubiquitous in Europe in the first half of the 19th century. They dominated the opera-houses of Germany, even while Goethe and Schiller were pursuing their high ideals for the theatre. But a land which had inherited *Die Zauberflöte* and *Fidelio*, and opened romantic vistas with *Der Freischütz* and *Oberon*, could not indefinitely submerge its national character. When Wagner had finished his work he had also given Germany a musical self-consciousness rooted in the legendary past as well as in the symphonic tradition of Beethoven. The very completeness of his achievement, like that of Verdi's in Italy, precluded anything but imitation or reaction. The approach to opera was more deliberately nationalist in Russia, who first found her own natural expression in music when Glinka and Dargomijsky turned attention from Italian opera to native themes and song. Consciousness of the Russian people as such was strong in both her music and literature. In Mussorgsky's *Boris Godunov*, the "people" in fact are a protagonist in the drama as much as Boris himself. In the operas of Rimsky Korsakov and in the *Firebird* ballet of Stravinsky, where human and supernatural elements are shown in interplay, chromaticism is the medium for magic, while folk-melody is used as the natural language of humanity—a humanity as yet untouched by Western politics and industrialism.

Far different was the situation in France, where Napoleon's Empire had grown out of the chaos of revolution. Political propaganda demanded heroic themes from Roman history, and a return to the noble austerity of the architecture of ancient Greece. Public taste preferred scenes of common life, subjects of sentimental appeal, and the emotional thrills of horror and rescue operas. Spectacle, noise, bombast, and artificial sentiment were the first fruits of liberty, equality, fraternity. France had to wait until the humiliation of her defeat by Bismarck in 1870 before she recovered her true self. From the second quarter of the century, the example of Spontini, Rossini, and Meyerbeer set the tone of "Grand Opera", centred on Paris but popular in all the opera-houses of Europe. It was designed for the entertainment of the pit and gallery as well as the newly-rich, a miscellaneous society seeing its own image not in the exalted figures and moods of the old *opera seria*, but in all human types and experiences, emotionalized by all the lavish resources of music and the stage. In the large and uneven output which continued throughout the century to meet this public demand, some works stand out with individual character: Gounod's *Faust*, Thomas' *Mignon*, Bizet's *Carmen* are familiar survivals. At the end of the century, the operas of Puccini and Richard Strauss had joined the stream, by now completely international. Along with it, the endless commentary on the comedy of life persisted, in *opéra comique* by Auber, in the ironic pleasantries of Offenbach's light operas, in the popular operettas of Johann Strauss, and of Gilbert and Sullivan in England.

In general, this mass of music had no high-flying aim as art; it was produced as entertainment, like opera in the past. Its interest for our present survey lies in its reflection of the public mind, especially in subsequent developments of the present century. The line of descent is unbroken, to Musical Comedy and Variety, to the fare provided in the vast bulk of broadcasting and television, and to the musical hits of youths who became famous on juke-boxes overnight. The history of music from the beginning has been one of popular as well as cultivated art. The man in the street, or in the medieval market-place, or in the Roman circus, is a permanent member of society. Whether any of the present popular activity can contribute a fertilizing influence as popular art did in the past can be left to speculation. Jazz rhythms and Negro melody have played a certain part, in sophisticated as in commercial music, but they sprang after all from folk-music, which was in essentials art-music, although its authors have remained unknown. Its germinal motives came at some stage from creative minds, and underwent a process of artistic shaping whether by one or many minds. Its thoughts and symbolism too were rooted deeply in the basic experiences of humanity, and conceived by people living in direct contact with nature. This was a living art, and a strangely compelling expression of the human mind and heart. It could not fail to permeate the work of other creative artists, whatever their degree of cultivation. It is difficult to see anything of this quality in the mass entertainment of to-day.

There seems then to be an unbridgeable gulf between any work of true artistic impulse and the degrading inanities which vast commercial organizations disseminate with a cynical contempt for values. Serious composers of opera in the 20th century have gone their own way, just as other contemporary artists, in exploring problems of their art regardless of immediate public reaction. Two opposite approaches to operatic form appear for example in the continuous texture of Debussy's *Pelléas et Mélisande* (1902) or Schönberg's *Erwartung* (produced 1924) on the one hand, and Stravinsky's return, on the other, to the 18th-century convention of separate arias in *The Rake's Progress* (1951), or in his still more stylized and static treatment of Jean Cocteau's *Oedipus Rex* (1927). Many new and difficult harmonic idioms, or experiments like *sprechgesang*, with its compromise between song and speech, restrict all these adventures to a public which is at present minute. Both in these technical matters, and in new ranges of subject, 20th-century opera reflects the modern attitude in its almost scientific probing of the realities of life. No aspect of unbalanced mind or sordid circumstance is excluded from this scrutiny, an austere reaction to man as he exists in reality, not as he has usually chosen to regard himself with varying degrees of sentiment or idealization. Whether such a work as Alban Berg's *Wozzeck* (1925) will ever make its impact on more than an artistically sensitive minority raises the eternal question of the function of art. For some, artistic experience is an end in itself, no matter what prompts its creation. For others it has always involved interpretation of life in terms of an ideal; and for others again, a mere pleasurable sensation and an escape from the pressing realities of existence. There is little doubt about what it means to the majority in an industrial age.

II

Industrialism is a product of the European mind and an example of its tendency to apply pure knowledge to practical uses. We enjoy its amenities and endure its abominations; it looms large for us in the 20th century, but this is due to its social effects, not to its intrinsic value for civilization. Mechanical, electrical, and atomic resources are only by-products of scientific discovery. The higher achievements of thought and imagination are those of pure science, not of its application to mere processes of everyday existence. Theories of political economy too, which accompanied the Industrial Revolution have no permanent interest; they served a temporary purpose just as the idea of the divine right of kings had done in an earlier phase. Thus, the utilitarian writings of Bentham, J. S. Mill, and Herbert Spencer have for the most part passed into oblivion, although Spencer (1820–1903) achieved a certain international eminence with his optimistic synthesis of the current findings of rationalist and evolutionary thought. Certain practical reminders remain: Bentham's principle of "the greatest happiness of the greatest number", and Malthus's gloomy warnings about the nemesis of over-population. With John Stuart Mill there emerged an awareness, gaining strength in many different quarters, that a problem does exist in finding outlets for the aspirations of the individual in the ruthless environment of industrial society. It is from this awareness, and from the reactions of humanity to the vast mechanical transformation of its way of life, that some living issues of the present have arisen. It is one of the misfortunes of mankind that industrialism developed with such scant regard for either human or aesthetic considerations. The callous use of labour engendered a class-antagonism which now is exploited to vitiate industrial relations long after its justification has been removed. The *laissez-faire* of the "Manchester School" of the 19th century stands condemned by all, but the tireless effort and humanitarian idealism of countless men and women attests the presence of a sense of individual responsibility on which the conception of democracy must rest. Indignation against the inhumanity of man to man took another form in the emergence of Socialist and Communist movements which seek to transfer this responsibility from the individual to the state. The opposition of these two views represents, at its best, a conflict of ideals, at its worst, a struggle for power.

Besides class-hostility, industrialism has bequeathed to us another deep-seated evil in the hideous sprawl of ugliness over town and countryside. This is a new situation, unparalleled in history. Art was always an indispensable adjunct of worship, as it was of princely prestige, but power which rests on the basis of industrial production does not depend on splendour and beauty. Indeed, for those who think only in terms of efficiency, beauty which already exists must be sacrificed to any material need. It is an irony of history that in the 19th century, when an unprecedented amount of building was needed, there was widespread indifference to all that is comely. Where impressive appearance was felt to be necessary, as in the façades of railway-stations and public buildings, imitation of older styles seemed to practical men to be the safest course—revivals of Greek, and Gothic and Baroque are strewn about our cities, and superimposed ornamentation betrays the absence of taste. Some prominent business firms are showing a more enlightened attitude to-day in sponsoring artistic effort untrammelled by any external dictates of taste. But the vast tracts of squalor remain, and the endless spread of concrete continues. Strangely enough, this flexible medium of structure offers a hope of a possible integration of art with practical life in the 20th century. Through the use of reinforced concrete, the architect is no longer restricted to the forms dictated by stone and brick. He can give to his materials whatever shape his imagination dictates—from lamp-standards, ugly or beautiful, to Festival Halls and fanciful creations like the new Opera House at Sydney, Australia (Plate 21). A feeling of opportunity and challenge is apparent among creative architects, whose work is bound up with the needs of society, and there is no lack of vision among those who see the hope of replacing dark satanic mills by creations of artistic inspiration. The task would be easier if this vision and hope were shared by the public who are now the rulers of society.

There are two weaknesses which seem to be inherent in the industrial system itself, apart from the unfortunate legacy of its early misguided development. The first is the assumption that expansion is inevitable, that to stand still is to fail in the struggle for existence. This is apparent in national and international politics, as well as in the separate units of industry. Economical use of machinery demands mass-production, large and ever larger markets, further extension of factories, and so on in a vicious circle. Since the infection has spread to the peoples of the East, with their fantastically increasing populations, the problem assumes ridiculous and alarming proportions. The second weakness arises from the practice of mass-production: machine-made articles replace the craftsman's work. At the best, with attention to good design in an age increasingly aware of this quality, individuality is lost both in the product and in the worker engaged in a routine process. At the worst, cheap and nasty goods add their influence to the squalid environment in which the majority of people exist. The spread of purchasing power, moreover, ensures a vast demand for goods among these people, and this, added to the universal parliamentary vote, brings to bear a political and economic pressure which is quite new in the affairs of mankind.

What connexion can there be between an artist's vision and a machine-conditioned public mind? It seems inevitable that he should withdraw into his private world of art. But was his work ever produced for the uneducated populace? Even when he was supported by a patron, he followed his own convictions in interpreting the demands made by his age. Now, when there is no prevailing motive or belief to give direction to his work, he is free as never before to go his own way, to treat what subjects he wishes, and make his technical innovations. He is not necessarily withdrawing from dreary material surroundings. Music in any case had reached a turning point by the end of the 19th century, a saturation point as far as old techniques were concerned. The visual arts had done so a generation before. The painters who exhibited in the *Salon des refusés* were not rebelling against external conditions of life, they were beginning to take fresh stock of the principles of their art. Musicians are likewise exploring new possibilities in organizing sounds, timbres, and rhythms whose significance is often purely structural. Stravinsky, Schönberg, Webern, and Bartók have given plenty of evidence of this attitude, and electronic experiments continue the process. Having assimilated their new techniques, composers can apply them to expressive purposes, as Schönberg does in his violin concerto. To many listeners the language may be foreign, but the fact of musical feeling is apparent. Younger listeners, growing up with these new orderings of sound, absorb them unconsciously as they do their native tongue; the gramophone and educational facilities assist the process. In this reorientation of music therefore, the composer is plotting his own personal course; the public must be left to follow as well as it can.

III

In science, from the time of the ancient Greeks until the establishment of experimental method in the 16th and 17th centuries, speculative thought had prevailed over factual observation. Man was the central point of reference in all this thought, and even in his worship he created God in his own image. The first phase of modern science gave him a sense of proportion about the earth's place in the universe. In the succeeding phase, man has learnt that the physical laws which govern the universe apply equally to him, and the sciences of geology, biology, astronomy, and atomic physics have shown him to be a speck in the infinity of time and space. The individual contributions to this edifice of knowledge are too numerous and too technical to recount; in themselves and in their sum they represent a triumph of intellect and imagination. These qualities are present in such high degree for example in the conception by Albert Einstein (1879–1955) of the space-time continuum, as to suggest a parallel with artistic intuition. Does not this great synthesis, expounded in mathematical terms, arise from the same qualities which caused the conception of a Gothic cathedral to be embodied in stone? or Bach's *Art of Fugue* to be created in sound? The answer lies in the word "created". It is no belittlement of the genius of Einstein to say that he is describing what actually occurs, not making a new creation. No scientist ever claims to do more than that, to describe in terms of current knowledge and thought the events of the physical universe. It is for the artist "to give to aery nothing a local habitation and a name".

Creation means life. The theory of Evolution set forth by Charles Darwin (1809–82) in his *Origin of Species* in 1859 shocked orthodox opinion in showing how close to "nature red in tooth and claw" is the life of man himself, and it provoked embittered controversy in the 1880's. The theories of Sigmund Freud (1856–1939) and the cognate ones of Jung and Adler, called further attention to the animal element in human nature, and they have had a far-reaching influence in the present century. Although they have no proven scientific foundation, they can have a salutory effect in focusing attention on the dual nature of man—the very fact with which religions have been concerned, and the very source of all creative impulse. It is not fanciful to trace some of the dark imaginings of the Romantic spirit to these regions of the unconscious, where deeply buried memories and impulses of animal nature exist at a different level from the reasoning faculties of the mind. Some philosophic systems of the 19th century began to take account of these less rational elements which affect man's relation to the world. Schopenhauer (1788–1860), significantly, influenced by Romantic and Indian thought, held that will is behind all phenomena, but that this cosmic will is the source of suffering; it is only by breaking down his individual will that man can attain equilibrium. Nietzsche (1844–1900) took the opposite view; his is not a philosophy of renunciation, but of powerful assertion of the individual will by the "superman" who despises the Christian virtue of meekness. Bergson (1859–1941) with his "élan vital" or life-force, and Benedetto Croce (1866–19—), for whom reality is a perpetual becoming, reflect the evolutionary trend, and the Americans William James and John Dewey lean to the practical application of thought, with emphasis on psychological and educational processes. (The psychological dramas of Ibsen (1828–1906) exercised considerable influence in the same direction, in the revelation of the hidden motives of conduct.) These broader interpretations of the mind of man and of his relationships to the world have moved a long way from the abstract logical systems of idealist philosophy. Fichte, at the opening of the 19th century, found it possible to argue that the Ego is the only ultimate reality—a conception nevertheless in which he contrived to include the idea of German national egoism. Hegel (1770–1831), by verbal logic again, persuaded himself that the opposite was true, that nothing is real except the whole, the Absolute. Subordinating natural will to this universal principle, he provided a basis for totalitarian beliefs, whose practical outcome the world has had opportunity to observe. His thought provided a basis for that of Karl Marx (1818–83), for whom classes, not nations, were the counters in the logical game.

The academic speculations of philosophers continue. But there is more hope in a search for truth which abandons *a priori* reasoning about the universe as a whole, and aims at solutions of specific isolated problems. This is the position of Bertrand Russell (born 1889), whose approach is through the practical sciences of physics and psychology. His phrase "a complex of compresences" conveys the idea of interrelation, which is inseparable from experience. The scientist, for whom nothing is constant but the velocity of light, observes and records relationships in the physical world and makes no dogmatic statement; the psychologist and teacher aim to bring greater harmony into human relationships; the religious believer aspires to a transcendental harmony; and the artist's task is to sublimate the experiences of mankind, with their inseparable elements of thought and feeling, into a harmony of significant beauty.

Index

DATE DUE
